Music, Spirit
and the
Keys to Prophecy

By
R.S. James

Sacred Scales
Denver, Colorado
www.sacredscales.com

Scripture quotations in this book are from the New King James Version of the Bible.

Music, Spirit, and the Keys to Prophecy
First Edition

Copyright © 2001 by R.S. James

All rights reserved. No portion of this book may be reproduced in any form, except for brief quotations in reviews (or as may be authorized in the "Notice to the 'truth censors'" section), without the written permission of the publisher.

February 2002, Sacred Scales.

ISBN 0-9710772-0-7
Bar-code intentionally omitted from cover art

Library of Congress Catalog Card Number: 2001117897

Printed in the United States of America

Table of Contents

Acknowledgments	4
Endorsements	5
Preface	7
Introduction	13
1. The Ancients	17
2. The Power to Heal	33
3. Inspiration: The Divine Process	39
4. Musical Tonality: The Fingerprint of God	47
5. The Musical Priesthood	71
6. The Music of the Prophets	83
7. Traditions: Of Men, of God	107
8. The Sacred Name of God	115
9. Music and the End-Times	129
10. Modern Music: The Battlefield	157

Appendices:
    I - The Creation: A Musical 'Midrash'   *179*
    II - The Biblical Fugue: How it all plays   *185*
        -An Eternal Ethic   *191*
    Glossary of Musical Terms   *193*

Acknowledgements:

In memory and appreciation of my parents for their self-sacrifice, love, and support of music and the spiritual calling.

Thanks to John Wheeler for the Music of the Bible illustrations and Ruth Boulee for her editorial expertise. The author also extends his thanks to all who helped by providing their support and encouragement during the writing of this book. To the biblical prophets and their spiritual lineage, who faithfully transmitted all that was given them from the hand of God, and to all those who labor to make the world a better place through music *without* selling out.

To the glory of the one true God and Creative Source ישוע המשיח Jesus, the Christ.

Endorsements:

"The question of what is appropriate in music has been intensely debated throughout human history. Nowhere has this been more true than in professing Christian circles . . . Author and professional musician/composer R.S. James steps into this arena with a novel approach. In *Music, Spirit, and the Keys to Prophecy*, he deals with the history and purpose of music from a biblical perspective and develops an intriguing model of how the tonal relationships in the diatonic octave (the acoustical and psychoacoustical foundation of musical sound) mirror historical and prophetic events as the Bible describes them. John Wheeler, *King David's Harp, Inc.*, Houston, TX.

"As each of us travels through the journeys of life, we encounter individuals who touch us with varying degrees of intensity. Those who freely give of themselves create the ultimate impact . . . R.S. James represents the love and spirit of Jesus Christ as he weaves his writings into a tapestry of history, wisdom and prophecy. Mr. James also brings the ancient biblical music into a NOW event." L. Scott Martin, Ph.D., *Academy of the Arts*, Denver, CO.

את

Jesus, in addressing His following concerning John the Baptist, rhetorically asked, "What did you go out into the wilderness to see? *A reed shaken by the wind?*" (Matt. 11:7) Using biblical imagery He was in effect saying, "did you think that John the Baptist is a false prophet swayed by modern teachings (i.e., winds of doctrine)?" Of course the correct answer was no, he was "a prophet . . . and more than a prophet." May that spirit, in some measure, be reflected in the pages of this book.

Preface

I began my musical studies as a youth with jazz piano lessons, learning the sublime art of improvisation, or 'spontaneous composition.' Then, going to college on a performing arts scholarship, I studied classical music, thus learning of the great improvisers of the past. I also had the opportunity of performing with small jazz ensembles. Later I entered the strange world of professional music, and worked in most of the modern idioms over a period of the next fifteen years.

The great and elusive mystery of music, however, was yet a wonder to me. What was its essence, why and how does it work, and what ultimately does it mean?

At age thirty I reached a turning point, coming to the end of myself through the various circumstances of life, I turned to spirituality for an answer. It was here that I began a relationship with the God of the Bible. I withdrew somewhat from the music profession and began studies relevant to my new faith. The Bible, history, the Hebrew language, and prophecy became my keen interests.

Over time I entered into several courses of study, as detailed in this book, which revolutionized my outlook on both music and my faith. I had developed a sense that the theologians had overlooked the importance of the arts and that the arts had attempted to exist independently of God. By re-integrating the two fields of study, I found that a clearer vision of both resulted. Books began to 'fall off the shelf' that corroborated this new approach.

New discoveries linking the musical art and biblical spirituality were becoming commonplace, yet I found one instance to be particularly stunning. Over a holiday break I had devoted time to complete a rough draft of this manuscript. In pursuing a theory connecting musical tonality to the themes of history and the Bible, I received an exciting breakthrough.

The theory was, upon closer study, proving itself out in the minutest detail. It appeared that I had discovered what no music theorist or Bible scholar had ever documented, or theorized, that the very physics of musical tonality indeed play themselves out in the major dramas of the Bible! Conversely, every piece of music, in its use of tonal physics, symbolically plays out the dramatic themes of the scriptures. This was what made for musical drama! I literally paused to catch my breath and let the grandeur of the idea settle in. Over the next few weeks, I was able to absorb and further corroborate these findings. Next was the matter of documenting and finalizing the manuscript. This book, however, had taken on a new and unimagined dimension.

Ultimately, I was satisfied that my long sought questions had been answered; of what the fundamental nature of music is, of why it works, and of what it means. I had simultaneously gained historic new insights into the drama of the Bible, of history, and of the prophecies that may be witnessed within our very lives.

What follows is the documentation of these findings and of what promises to be a new and more comprehensive approach to both music appreciation and biblical studies.

Submission and Independent Research

"See, I have this day set you over the nations and over the kingdoms, to root out and to pull down, to destroy and to throw down, to build and to plant." Jer. 1:10.

Prior to any act of restoration comes the labor of analyzing the inventory and dismantling the unusable goods. While this is not always a pleasant task, it is one that is necessary in order to reap the harvest of a new planting. One may thus find cause to take offense with some of the material presented in the following pages. This is not intended, neither is it particularly avoided. Those who hold to religious and cultural traditions *above* reasoned truth are at particular risk here. Honest assessments and a non-compromising approach to the subject matter have gleaned a harvest of new revelation. Be assured, the novelty and depth of content found within these pages will be worth the risk of a few 'sacred cows' to anyone who takes the journey.

End-time culture Scripture tells us that the time leading to the return of Christ will be marked by deception and even delusion. Christ warned of those who would " . . . deceive, if possible, even the elect." (Matt.24:24). The apostle Paul prophesied, "because they did not receive the love of the truth, . . . God will send them strong delusion, that they should believe the lie," (2Thess. 2:10-11). Our generation, more than any other, should therefore be willing to examine our assumptions and rigorously test and prove *all things* by the Word of truth.

The issue of what constitutes revelation from God is an essential, and yet politically volatile issue. While many today claim to be delivering new truth, and some the only truth, such claims most often do not stand up to close scrutiny. It seems that it is all too easy for one to write a book that claims new revelation, to include a requisite number of scriptural references, and promote the package to a large audience of ill-informed people. Carefully documented scholarship is more difficult to produce, and much more difficult to market, especially in today's fast-paced society.

The issue of *correct* submission to rightful authority is therefore fundamental to that of true scholarship. Incorrect submission is a state of compromise with the truth involving non-biblical traditions (which as we shall see are still ingrained in religious cultures today), authorities not God-ordained, those with stated yet not demonstrated gifting, conclusions reached by group consensus outside of biblical procedure (peer pressure), and to all manner of self-conceits. Correct submission involves being in agreement with Scripture, the Holy Spirit (spirit of truth), true historical data, experts in related fields of study, and all such principles of 'checking.' This latter approach is what provides the 'rubbing' effect necessary to refine and sift through the revelations that may come to one working independent of the compromised academic and religious institutions of today.

Additionally, different levels of scriptural interpretation may be applied. Jewish rabbis describe these in terms of the *p'shat*, or simple reading, the *derash*, or inductive, and the *sod*, or hidden. Such interpretations may offer one deeper insight into a particular verse, but no scripture should ever be in conflict with any another that addresses the same subject.

As a subtext to the development of this work, I would add something that I have increasingly observed in the realm of professional music. Although historically, the serious musician has worked against the odds to produce his art, the cultural climate of today is particularly distressing. In both religious and secular communities there is a growing disrespect of the musical art. In some cases this is expressed directly, yet more often and just as damaging, indirectly. In not distinguishing the gifted, or by doing so but failing to provide just compensation for those that are put into service, the spirit that music can carry is stifled. One does not use other professionals in such a way. Dentists, lawyers, builders, or computer programmers are not asked to prepare during the week and perform free of charge on the weekend, as a matter of course. But this is increasingly the situation of the studied musician today. Lectures are given from the pulpit about musician's careers in the secular realm and of their participation in the evils of the entertainment industry. A true "Catch 22." While there are a variety of reasons for such attitudes, as will be herein discussed, it is hoped that this work will provide a means of correction, demonstrating that music, in addition to being a culturally significant profession, is also an essential biblical and prophetic ministry. And to ask, as did reformist Martin Luther, "Why should the Devil have all the good music?"

Notice to the "truth censors." As some of the information in this book may be a threat to those who profit from the suppression of truth, the author has taken appropriate precautions. Prior to publication, trustworthy individuals were given the means to widely distribute this edition of *Music, Spirit, and the Keys to Prophecy*. Should any significant harm befall the author, or should the author or publisher be significantly hindered from the publication or distribution of *Music, Spirit, and the Keys to Prophecy*, these individuals will provide their contacts with the keys to decrypt the work for worldwide distribution. Copyright permission shall be irrevocable upon the author's untimely demise or the implementation of the "mark of the beast" when, during the Great Tribulation, commerce will require one's bowing to 666.

Introduction

Living in a time and culture that offers at once the very best and the worst of everything for our amusement, it is easy to become complacent in our responses to the various stimuli of life. In no area is this truer than the musical arts.

Running as a continuous drone in the background of our lives, rhythmic cadences punctuate and persuade our every movement in modern society. Recorded music and video technology accompany virtually every shopping trip, social event and commute. The electronic media that is now omnipresent in the public square only grudgingly gives way to live performance and even less to silence. The musical taste of others, or more often the lack thereof, thus bombards us at every turn. In addition to which, electronic bells and beeps, buzzers and horns command our attention and relentlessly prompt our responses. A musical form of 'road rage' stalks the streets as youths drive their cars with powerful sub-bass stereos which blast their profanities, destroying any remnant of a peaceful ambience. All such modern abuses add emphasis to the old axiom that "silence is golden," and oh, so rare.

However, beneath the abuses and excesses lies a force that if properly understood and utilized, may heal, inspire, and even carry the oracles of God, able to pierce into the deepest recesses of the human soul and spirit. With this intrinsic sacred quality being lost on many today, we must evaluate and refine our views, and seek to re-establish the ancient and true standards that guard and support the musical form of expression.

Herein is the battleground for the soul of a culture and a people, of what message is worthy of adornment by this most sublime of human expressions. Will it be the ever-degrading messages of the popular culture, or will a people of principal and faith raise a standard and give their message the most persuasive of presentations?

The following pages contain a compelling account of the nature of this battle, through the pages of history, the sacred texts, and the study of the art of music itself. The material presented will awaken the reader to a part of himself either dormant or dulled by the various abuses within the cultural and religious traditions. Whether performer or listener, teacher or student, the material in this volume will help one understand connections and context that have escaped studied people to date and bring one's appreciation of this vital force to a new and unimagined level.

This book will help to establish truths that have been neglected and lost, and some that have never before been documented. It will portray the reality of music as the perfect allegory for the spiritual life, one inextricably woven throughout the pages of history and the scriptures; that it is primarily about a conveyance of intimacy, uniquely joining its audience and its message. (This is greatly evidenced by the strong reactions that occur when one proposes to set any standards for the genre). Further, it will demonstrate how the Bible, as the ultimate Script for the human drama, by the ultimate Author, contains the ultimate musical score and poetry, and in the New Testament the ultimate Redemption and Finale-the Revelation. That music is a true 'Holy Grail' of scriptural interpretation, for both the Old and New Testament. And beyond this is something that none have yet observed, that the dramatic template for history and the Bible itself is to be found in the very physics of the musical scale.

1

The Ancients

"And they have caused themselves to stumble in their ways, from the ancient paths" Jer. 18:15

Perhaps no better social barometer exists within a given culture than that of the musical arts. Throughout the pages of history the ultimate defining symbol of a society is arguably its musical and cultural legacy. The ancient cultures, whether pagan or monotheistic, esteemed music above all as a spiritual or cosmic force. Music was seen as the ultimate reflection of the Divine Order, as that which spoke of science and morality, math, nature, and philosophy. It has been seen as perhaps the single greatest force within any culture to instruct and to unify people of conscience. In short, throughout the pages of history, great cultures produced great music.

These concepts may be difficult for the modern man as we now think in uniquely compartmentalized terms. Every field of endeavor has become separate unto itself, none connecting to the other and, more frequently, none connecting to God. Such heresies would have been unheard of in the greater ancient cultures.

This process of fragmentation is one that has taken place noticeably in more recent history. It was the nineteenth century, with its industrial revolution, the humanistic movements in the arts, and the development of 'scientific inquiry,' that was the main point of departure from the ancient understandings. It was also the cultural catalyst leading to the present time, which is now seeing the fruit of an almost complete break from the path that defined western life prior to the nineteenth century.

We may also trace a societal departure from the ancient God of the Bible through the parallel developments in philosophy beginning in the nineteenth century. What began as *humanism* (serving humanity as the dominant ethic) was the seed for twentieth century *nihilism* (there are no ethics), and has become *post-modernism* (self-created ethics) by the start of the twenty-first century. This last view is by far the most toxic, as it allows one to rationalize any form of evil, entirely removing the need for external referencing on issues of moral conduct.

Indeed, this philosophy was anticipated by the Apostle Paul who warned that in the last days, before the return of Christ, men would be " . . . lovers of themselves, lovers of money, boasters, proud, blasphemers, disobedient to parents, unthankful, unholy, unloving, unforgiving, slanderers, without self-control, brutal, despisers of good, traitors, headstrong, haughty, lovers of pleasure rather than lovers of God, having a form of godliness but denying its power. And from such people turn away!" (2Tim. 3:3-4).

Parallel Movements in the Arts
The departure from the Ancient Path

Music	Philosophy	View	Traits
18th Century Baroque/Classical.	Ancient Path (connectedness)	Art serves God	Intellect over emotion
19th Century Romantic	Humanism 'Man' centered	Worship of art & artist	Emotion over intellect
20th Century Atonal/12-Tone	Nihilism	There is no God, ethics	Chaotic, break from tonality
1950-present Degraded pop forms. End of western art-music tradition	Post Modernism (fragmentation)	Self is God.	Selfishness. No sense of community. Pleasure-seeking

Philosophy, according to its name, "the love of wisdom," has lost all its historic bearings and governing principles. Scripture, which the modern world has through its ignorance overlooked or outright rejected, maintains that the beginning of wisdom is the "fear of the Lord" (Prov. 9:10). It is no wonder then that a basic crises of being exists for so many in our culture today.

The humanism of the nineteenth century spawned an interesting theological offspring as well, that of the 'Pre-Tribulational rapture' theory. Co-existing in harmony with humanistic philosophy, this departure from historic Christian teaching asserted that the church will not experience the difficulties that precede the second coming of Christ; rather, it will escape by means of a (humanitarian) rapture. The theory, popularized by theologian John Darby in the mid-eighteenth century,[1] has by now become an almost unquestioned doctrine of the evangelical church, to the point of being a requisite for anyone wishing a staff or teaching position in such organizations. It also was the vehicle for humanist philosophy as it made its way into the Christian church, and a prophetic catalyst that helped to move us from the ancient, God-centered path, to a more popular man-centered one.

The effects of this view of the rapture are contrary to the teachings of historical Christianity. Instead of the conversion experience being viewed as the *beginning* of a purifying walk with the one true God, the pre-Tribulation rapture suggests to its followers that conversion is the *culmination* of the spiritual experience, and that one only need to wait upon a final escape from the world's problems to have their ultimate union with God. Suffering and sacrifice often accompanied belief in Christ in past eras, and served as a means of testing and purifying one's faith. Yet this is seemingly out-dated for the adherents of this end-time doctrine. It also appears to breed complacency among Christians who would rather remain comfortable and ignorant, than develop discernment and separate from the beastly system of Mystery Babylon which, as even they will admit, now appears to be manifesting itself.

A pre-Tribulation rapture, perhaps most importantly, does not fit the dramatic template of the Bible in which the theme of 'ascension' always occurs at week's end. (This will be fully demonstrated in chapters 4&9). As the beginning of the Tribulation does not coincide with the end of another biblical 'week,' the rapture can only, therefore, be at the end of the seven-year Tribulation. The coincidental timing of the related ideas of humanist

---

[1] Ice, Thomas D. *The Origin of the Pretribulation Rapture*, Part II Biblical Perspectives, Vol. II, No. 2 Biblical Perspectives, Austin, TX Mar/ Apr. 1989 p.5.

philosophy and the pre-Tribulation rapture theory alone, however, should raise some serious questions for the astute observer of history.

Further fragmentation has found its way into the modern Church as well. Through a ritualized watering down of the Gospel message, a focus on *conversion to* rather than *discipleship in* the faith (see the "Great Commission" of Matt. 28:19), and an overemphasis on the practice of preaching, the Christian community has become virtually indistinguishable from the secular. Statistics on divorce, abortion, and other moral indicators readily bear this out. An advocate and practitioner of Christian discipleship in the early twentieth century, Oxford Group founder Frank Buckman likened preaching to "throwing eye medicine on to a crowd from a second story window" and emphasized instead, a more intimate one on one approach, which he called "soul surgery."

True fellowship and intimacy are inhibited by the structure of the meetings and by the redundant focus on the elementary doctrines of the faith. Replayed weekly like a sacred mantra the new convert remains immature as the *milk* of the Word seldom gives way to solid food. One may easily experience years of church[1] attendance without ever engaging in close, meaningful contact with others. The all-important weekly gatherings, mostly dominated by events and personalities on the podium, may at best open to five minutes of time to "greet your neighbor."[2] This hardly creates the kind of atmosphere that allows for the confessing of weaknesses, for encouragements, for rebukes, or personal prayer (2Tim. 4:2). It is not surprising, then, that unresolved sins remain covered up and unchecked for years, and even lifetimes. Truly, we seem at times to be

---

[1] The term church, or "ecclesia," simply means "the called out ones," or "assembly".
[2] Not to downplay the importance of liturgy, however it is the aspect of community that is wanting in the American church today.

brought into the middle of the battle and then are left without the training and equipment with which to fight.

Many church-goers of today have difficulty speaking in the first-person regarding spiritual experience. One must listen to the recounting of what such and such a pastor says, or this tape or that speaker in order to receive a spiritual point. Quoting scripture as an abstract, without a personal realization of its truths, is a transparent and ineffective device, but is in wide use nonetheless. Such spirituality cannot be attractive to the outsider, if the life of the congregant isn't more deeply penetrated.

The twelve-step recovery movement, which has gained prominence over the course of the last century, carries the basic discipleship principles of the biblical faith better than many religious denominations of today, yet is itself variously flawed. As a departure from the Oxford Group's 'first century Christianity,' the twelve-step movement incorporated many correct spiritual disciplines, yet has increasingly removed the focus from being that of the biblical Christ. Here, one may experience the healing principles of self-surrender, open sharing, confession of sins, restored relationships, and freedom from a dogmatic hierarchal structure, but is discouraged from seeking and proclaiming faith in the one true God. As a further example of fragmentation there is now a twelve-step group for virtually every possible sin habit, or 'addiction.' None, however, name their problem as 'sin,' or deal with the sin condition in general.

People in modern society are also isolated by their access to a vast array of choices. The average individual has personal entertainment available at his command in the form of televisions, car stereos, walkmans, PC's and the like. Stores are stocked with products from every type of artist and medium imaginable. No longer is there a need to interact within a community to experience the arts. "You may choose whatever you will, just leave me alone with my choice," is the cry. The ethical and aesthetic principles involved in music and art are not considered today, only their potential to produce pleasure and most importantly, self-exaltation. These, too, would be heresies to any culture with any noble or enduring legacy.

There do exist, however, varying differences in cultural attitudes from one society to the next. The French tend to value academics and aesthetics, Americans money and power, and Latin cultures family unity, as an example; yet similar destructive trends are impacting all alike.

Musically speaking, a clear dividing line from the past may be drawn symbolically with the work of Ludwig von Beethoven. Not only was this composer the stylistic bridge from classical to romantic music (i.e. *Roman*tic), but he also expressed the revolt against subservience to the existing social order. An heir to the great musical traditions of Haydn and Mozart, he was a bridge to the future that was to come out of the French Revolution, in his attitude and his music. It was a shock to his hearer, for instance, when he proclaimed that an expected visit from royalty would favor not himself, but the visiting royal. After all, he explained, there are many royals, but "only one Beethoven." A plaster cast of his bust (an idolatrous symbol) was prominent throughout the 19th and 20th centuries and came to represent the "ultimate artist." This departure has indeed greatly impacted contemporary thought, in which *self*-expression has become the ultimate object of desire. In opposition to which, the Bible declares the objective to be a *crucified* self and the expressed Christ.

Beethoven's spiritual beliefs are interesting as well. His epic Ninth Symphony was written as a setting for a Schiller poem, and includes the famous "Ode to Joy" chorus:

> Praise to Joy the God descended
> Daughter of Elysium,
> Ray of mirth and rapture blended
> Goddess to thy shrine we come.
> By thy magic is united,
> What stern custom parted wide,
> All mankind are brothers plighted,
> Where thy gentle wings abide.[1]

This is definitely not the God of the Bible that J.S. Bach knew. This "descended" god (and goddess) uses magic to unite the "brotherhood of mankind," a favorite theme of freemasonry.

Richard Wagner wrote of Beethoven's Ninth, "A struggle . . . of the soul contending for happiness against the oppression of that inimical power which places itself between us and the joys of the earth."[2] What power could be seen as coming between man and the joys of the earth for Richard Wagner, and Beethoven, except the God of the Bible? This indeed is quite a departure from the Baroque and Classical ideals of reverence and piety.

Another significant departure that coincided with the Romantic era was that of the industrial revolution. Prior to the late eighteenth century, men interacted with the ecology, and thus the creation, in order to maintain their sustenance on earth. Since then, society has progressively become estranged from the natural environment, learning to exist in a dependant condition within a largely artificial world. The necessary skills for survival now involve

---

[1] Cross, Milton/Ewan, David. New York. *Encyclopedia of the Great Composers and Their Music.* Doubleday & Co., Inc. 1953 pg. 63.
[2] Ibid pg. 62.

manipulating technologies that are outside of our control, rather than interacting healthily within the natural universe. Despite the many material benefits, the price to our collective soul has been substantial.

Within the abundance that is available to the masses today, there is seen a toxic 'watering-down' of the necessary elements of life. Fast-foods that are void of nutrition, chemically treated water, unhealthy entertainment mediums, debased musical forms, and compromised spirituality flood the cultural landscape. We thus consume, yet are left empty, even to the point of desolation.

Given the condition of our culture today, we must then ask, "What is the way back?" If, indeed, there is a way.

The Ancient Path

It is the growing experience of many that our attitudes and actions in a variety of areas affect the overall quality of our lives. What we eat, what we watch and listen to, and what we think about all interact and have consequences on the whole. How we view sex affects how we view God, how we view art affects how we view others. A breakthrough in the area of diet, for instance, can help deepen one's spiritual life and effectiveness. A performance of great music teaches much about the spiritual life and elevates the spirit. Through silent, listening prayer God can still speak directly to a willing heart that is surrendered to Him. The ancient wisdom is thereby re-asserting itself among those wearied with the destructiveness of modern society.

In ancient times, the knowledge of God's deliverances and judgments in the earth, and thus His sovereignty, were well established within the various cultures. This came about through the retelling of the stories of His mighty works throughout the various generations of man. The Creation, Noah's flood, the judgments at Babel and Sodom, and the Exodus all have left their traces in the cultural legends of the earth. Historically, it was through these stories that all men were able to know of the relationship between cause and effect on the spiritual level, without the obfuscations and illusions created by modern political spin, media, and entertainment technology.

From the standpoint that the ancient cultures agreed on an interconnection between the various disciplines of life, of people to each other, and to God, the debate yet raged in another area. This had to do with which God or force was the prime Cause for all such experience. Was it the God of the pagans, or of the Hebrews? This same issue, in fact, rages all the more today. People are seeking to improve and understand their lives, and doing the same kinds of things to achieve these goals, but are yet divided when it comes to the fundamental issue of "who is God?"

Hebraism and Hellenism

In studying the pages of history, a major source of intrigue is found in the interplay that has occurred between the Gentile (Greek) and Hebraic (Jewish) cultures. Major events emanate from these two forces coming into relationship with each other and often, conflict. The Bible itself is evidence of this interchange, resting on thirty-nine books from the Hebrew language and twenty-seven in the Greek. Some today would attempt to oversimplify the subject by siding with one or the other, asserting that everything Hebraic is good and all things Hellenistic (Greek in origin) are evil, or vice-versa. The truth, however, is more subtle and complex, with a good bit of mixture being evident within both cultural traditions by now. Nineteenth century church historian Alfred Eidersheim traces the cultural and religious interchange as follows. According to the Jewish writer Aristobulus (160 B.C.), Pythagorus, Plato, and the other Greek sages learned their systems of ethics and philosophy from Moses and the Torah. These systems were adapted as pagan mythology without, however crediting their original source, the Hebrew Bible. The writing of the Septuagint (the Greek translation of the Bible) was the springboard for popular proliferation of the pagan myths by these Greek philosophers. The exchange continued as non-inspired Jewish writers adapted the Greek Hellenistic concepts back into the Hebrew language, via the Talmud, also without source-referencing the Greek philosophers they borrowed from.[1] The corruptions of the Greek writers thereby entered into Judaism and the Hebrew culture. In the course of these exchanges, truth and error became blended aspects of both cultural traditions.

It was against this backdrop that the revelation of the New Testament scriptures was given, inspired in Greek and resting on the Hebrew prophecies, as a summation and final resolution to the historic interchange. The purest form of truth, therefore, is now a harmonizing of the Hebrew "Old Testament" and the Greek "New Testament" revelation.[2]

---

[1] Eidersheim, Alfred. *The Life and Times of Jesus the Messiah*, Mass: Hendrickson Publishers, Inc. 1994, p.25-26.
[2] The traditional terms for the divisions of the Bible as Old and New Testament are misleading. As Cohen asserts, the former reflects on four major divine covenants (Edenic, Abrahamic, Mosaic, Jehoiachinic), and the latter three (Messianic, Millenial Reign, Eternal State). A better terminology would be 'Hebrew Scripture' and 'Greek Scripture.'

This is also now a closed or completed canon (Rev. 22:18-19). The Bible is thus representative of a God who desires to communicate to seekers of truth, both Jew and Gentile alike, and One, it must be said, with a strong sense of irony.

Some modern theories suggest that the New Testament is based on a lost Hebrew 'original' version. The arguments that support this theory are only speculative at best and have not addressed the mountain of evidence supporting the Greek text in order to be taken at all seriously. While it is true that the New Testament scriptures were written predominantly by Jewish writers and thereby contain many Hebraic cultural idioms, the internal as well as the manuscript evidence is overwhelmingly in favor of Greek being the original inspired language of the New Testament. Certainly we are far from exhausting what is recorded there in any event.

It is interesting to note as a modern continuation to this historic cultural interplay, the attempt within the Hollywood creative culture to break down the figurative 'middle wall of partition' between Jew and Gentile. This is something that may be evidenced in many of the themes of today's popular entertainment mediums.

One current example is the movie *Meet the Parents* starring Ben Stiller. This comedy revolves around a contemporary Jewish man who is seeking acceptance within the Gentile culture of his fiancé. The couple visits their future in-laws to establish a common ground socially as the story plays itself out through the implied awkwardness of the situation. The resolution to the drama comes in the form of a final breaking-down of barriers (middle wall) and the acceptance of each side's uniqueness. It is interesting that even on a subliminal level, the secular mediums inevitably strive towards a working out of the themes of the Bible. The reality of the situation, which Hollywood misses, is that barriers between people and groups may only truly be done away with through faith in the Messiah, and not with human efforts, no matter how cleverly conceived the plot (Eph. 2:14).

A Societal Force

Music has historically been a great unifying factor within human culture. It has been at the center of the life of civilized societies throughout history, setting the tone for ethics, morality, education, and national spirit. What today is called classical music was actually the product and possession of the various cultures that supported and influenced their respective artisans. The inspirations flowed both ways, from the culture to the artist and then back to the culture. It was none the less so within ancient Israel.

Throughout the pages of scripture, we see worship as central to the life of God's chosen nation. One striking account of this was the dedication of Solomon's Temple (2 Chron. 5:13). We are told that as the people of God were singing and playing in *unity*, the cloud (or presence) of God fell so powerfully that the musical priests could not even continue playing. This is an event that any religious leader today would greatly enjoy seeing repeated in his meetings, and it punctuates the importance of oneness amongst a people of faith, and the power of musical worship to accomplish that goal.

The function of music on the human psyche also takes on an interesting dimension. The word derives from the pagan 'Muses,' thought to be the daughters of 'Jove' and 'Memory.' The terms 'amusement' and 'jovial' owe their origin to these mythological characters.

Augustine, who was esteemed by the early church for his interest in music wrote that sound, "flows by into the past and is imprinted upon the memory," whereas intellect is "of the present."

It has been observed that adding melody to a verse of prose aids in the memorization process. Such an application however, is but one of the levels of the musical experience. Music actually has the ability to engage the senses as no other discipline can.

The memory in fact operates on three distinct levels. The first is the *motor or physical* part of playing that must be mastered. This involves learning the techniques necessary to perform a given piece: the scales, rhythms, and harmonic elements as applied to one's particular instrument or voice. The next is the *cognitive, or intellectual* aspect. Studying the theoretical and historical underpinnings of the selection is necessary for apprehension of this level. At this stage, we are concerned with organizational structures, form, tonal syntax and the like. The last is the *emotional and spiritual* realm without which the preceding two levels are but empty exercises. Here the student learns to convey the unseen and abstract intent of the composer, taking into consideration the various facts surrounding the piece, the period, the composer's life circumstances, style, beliefs and culture. These levels of expression then are transmitted to an audience through the vehicle of live performance.

The type of memories created by music are then not only stronger than those of a mere 'rote' variety, but are multi-dimensional, facilitating *experiential* memories: physical, emotional, cognitive, and also spiritual. Such an art is thereby unique, representing perhaps the most complete of experiences available on this side of eternity.

With this in mind, the reader may be gaining insight as to why music has been such a cultural battleground throughout history. He who utilizes such an expressive tool gains significantly in the battle of ideas and values.

Music with Prophecy

The playing of instruments in the Bible is often associated with prophesying or speaking forth the oracles of God (1Sam. 10:5). The prophet Samuel directed Saul, the future king of Israel, to meet musical prophets and to join them in prophesying. It was through this process that he would be changed into "a new man." The correlation is something to ponder. The playing of instruments here either facilitated, or even promulgated the presence and speaking forth of God's word, something far better understood in ancient times than modern, no doubt. It has been observed that whatever else was taught in these ancient 'schools of prophets,' music was an essential part.[1]

The disciplines of music and of the spiritual life are synonymous. The fact that both require the ability to deal in multi-dimensional subject matter may alone explain the linking of the two within the scriptures. Additionally, there is the need to be able to recognize patterns and to discern meaning and dramatic content.

Symbolism

Musical instruments carry with them interesting symbolism, historically and biblically. In ancient times, it was the carrying of a harp that distinguished the warrior victorious in battle. This symbolism is mimicked in 'coats of arms' representing lineal achievements, such as the Celtic harp in British heraldry, (although an occult art form,

---

[1] Exegesis Parallel Bible. Orange, CA: Exegeses 1994. p 425.

the renderings point to this ancient concept). It was thereby an ancient symbol of *freedom* and *victory* to possess and utilize musical instruments.

We see in the Psalms that a backslidden and *captive* Israel was moved to "hang up" their harps by the Babylonian rivers (Psalm 137:2), unable to respond to their captors' request to perform their national songs.[1] Conversely, in the Revelation, we see the 144,000 Israelites on Mount Zion and the saints who come out of the Tribulation playing harps to punctuate their *victory* over the kingdom of the Beast and Mystery Babylon (Rev. 14:2). Thus it is that freedom and musical worship are inseparable partners in the divine economy.

Biblical imagery consistently connects the harp with prophecy. The book of the Psalms, well known to have been accompanied songs, are among the most prophetic of the books of the Old Testament, and the Revelation makes use of this imagery in connection with prophecy and the delivery of the Oracles of God during the course of the Tribulation, i.e., the new song.

When taken as a whole, the Bible places music at the very heart of the spiritual life, and of the workings of the Almighty. This prominence should not be seen as mere allegory, or taken too lightly, as will soon be demonstrated.

---

[1] The ancient Hebrews were apparently well known for their musical expressions (Ps.137:3).

2

Power to Heal

"... that David would take a harp and play it with his hand. Then Saul would become refreshed and well ..."

The force of music is something that contains within itself definitive *spiritual power*, and throughout history this force has been known of and utilized. The ancient civilizations greatly revered music as a divine gift with powers commensurate to such its source. This reality is clearly seen in the biblical texts. When the young David was brought to play before king Saul (1Samuel 16:14-23), it was his *instrumental* music skills that were sought after and that ultimately drove out the evil spirit by which Saul was afflicted (i.e., healed him). Certain points are significant in this passage: 1) David was chosen because of his mastery of an instrument (the harp) . . . "Provide me now a man who can play well" (vs. 17). Not only was it apparent to Saul that music may be the answer to his ills, but it was known within the king's court that the young David was a skilled artisan. Although only a shepherd at the time, David was known even at the pinnacle of society for his music. 2) It was this very skill that precipitated a healing. By the law of kinds alone we know that it takes a spiritual force to conquer a spiritual force. The music that David was playing was instrumental, as there is no mention of singing. We must therefore conclude that music, when done well, has a kind of spiritual power. 3) This event was then successful in repetition. The affliction was recurrent and the cure was dependable, leaving Saul each time, refreshed (vs.23).

This exercise has of course been repeated throughout history. Most notable are the famous Goldberg Variations by J.S. Bach, which were written for their namesake, the harpsichordist of one Count Kaiserling. The pieces were to be played in a room adjacent to the Count's sleeping quarters in order to ease a case of insomnia. A direct replay, if you will, of the biblical story.

(Additionally, J.S. Bach, perhaps the most original and prolific of the great composers, characteristically began his compositions with the initials JJ, for *Jesu Juvah*, Latin meaning "help O Jesus." At the end would appear SDG, for *Soli Deo Gloria*, meaning "to God be all the glory."[1] These statements have been used as a means for authenticating his works, and are also confirmation as to the source of his greatly inspired music.)

Instrumental music uniquely embodies important properties that bear mentioning. As opposed to prose or songs, there are no words to interpret or misunderstand. Language by its very nature carries judgments and

---

[1] From *Bachfaq.org*. Bernard S. Greenberg. 1999.

discriminations that may or may not be properly received by its hearer, or properly delivered by its messenger. Not so with music. This form of expression is completely neutral in that sense. Who the hearer is and what he gets from the performance transcends the cognitive. Politics, class, race, and other such considerations are swept aside and the deeper, unspoken truths of life come to the fore. Music truly is "the universal language."

Musical expressions are also among the most pure and honest in all human endeavor. It is known within musical circles that it is virtually impossible to lie or deceive through one's instrument. That which is on the inside of the player, (passion, soul, 'feel'), is what comes through his instrument, never more, and this is recognizable (though perhaps in varying degrees) by all.

Touch

The Hebrew word used in scripture for play is *nogain*, from the root *nagan* meaning, 'to touch.' It is this word that is used today to describe the skilled instrumentalist, e.g., "the pianist played with a good *touch*." The word takes on a further meaning in the New Testament and is also connected with divine healing, although not necessarily through the means of a tonal device. Here the person of faith has himself become the 'instrument' of the Almighty, and his touch likewise has spiritual power. This is notably seen in the healing miracles of Christ, and those of the Apostles after the resurrection, being effective both for healing and the transmission of the Holy Spirit.

Clement of Alexandria wrote of this connection in *Exhortation to the Greeks*, likening the bodies of Christians to the strings of David's harp, and Jesus the musician playing hymns of praise to His father.[1]

(In light of this analogy, one might observe a virtuoso instrumental performance, asking himself if he is, or wills to be, as responsive to the Spirit of God as the instrument is to its performer, i.e., to let God play him as a finely tuned instrument!)

The effect that music has on the subconscious is a lengthy study all itself. Sympathetic vibration is the phenomenon that occurs when a string on an instrument is plucked. The adjacent strings, if unencumbered, will vibrate sympathetic to the frequency created by the principle string. The ancients believed this phenomenon occurred as well when an individual was hearing music, that one's soul would 'vibrate' to whatever modes and melodies were being played. They also theorized that the musician himself responds to a greater "music of the cosmos" as the entire universe was thought to vibrate harmoniously. It was believed that the mathematical ratios which govern the harmonic system, naturally producing a seven-tone scale, were also represented in the then seven known planets of our solar system, which themselves play the cosmic themes.

Whatever turns out to be the case, it is beyond question that music has a profound and sublime effect on the individual, operating at levels yet to be fully understood. Performer and audience alike know of the profound sense of spirituality to be gained from a good concert experience, and as such needs not be further explained here.

Those who have been fortunate enough to be associated with an exceptional artist can attest to the fact that these are

---

[1] James, Jamie. *Music of the Spheres.* New York: Copernicus Springer-Verlag, 1995, p.70.

among the most rare and stunning of individuals. Those with whom I have been privileged to interact have always left me somewhat awestruck not only by their art, but also by their extraordinary 'personas.' These relationships more than anything else cause one to persist through the rigors and hardships of the musical profession. Notwithstanding the proverbial eccentricities, there seems to be a heightened sensitivity to the things fundamental to life that one must possess in order to excel in the musical field. Any of the biographies written on the lives of great artists will also attest to these facts, and are well worth reading for inspirational purposes.

Given such qualities, we should not be surprised of the therapeutic effect to be gained by exposure to such a person's gifting on a sick soul, or a healthy one, for that matter.

Spirit and Sound

Within the many musical references in the Bible are those that draw a close parallel to, and in some cases do not distinguish at all between, the Lord and music. This connection is seen in Psalm 22:3, "But You are holy, who *inhabit* the praises of Israel."

In the Song of the Red Sea (Exodus 15:2), Moses and later Isaiah (Isaiah 12:2) proclaim God to be their "strength, *song* and . . . salvation." Beyond the obvious metaphor lies a deep truth, of a God who is so connected with this mode of expression that He literally is seen as one and the same, as the Divine Song itself.

Clement of Alexandria used music as a metaphor for Christ, describing Him as the New Song. "See how mighty is the New Song. They who were otherwise dead revived when they but heard the New Song."

The New Testament contains an interesting direct reference that has been largely overlooked. Christ is described as the *logos* of God, "In the beginning was the Word (*logos*)" (John 1:1). This is traditionally interpreted to mean the written word of the biblical text. The Greek word for ratio, however, is also *logos*. The seven-tone scale, as observed from ancient times to the present is based upon mathematical relationships, i.e., *ratios*. 1:2 an octave, 2:3 a fifth, 3:4 a fourth, and so on. Now consider the definition from Liddell and Scott's Greek-English Lexicon: "*Logos*-that by which the *inner thought* is expressed. Latin oratorio- the inward thought itself, Latin *ratio*." This expands the concept of logos from the traditionally understood, 'written word,' to a broader concept of, 'expressed thought.' It would not, therefore, be incorrect to render John 1:1, "In the beginning was the *Divine Expression*...and the *Divine Expression* was God." Music is truly a sublime means of expressing the inward thought, and the Bible, in the original Greek, connects it directly to Christ.

The ancient scientist, philosopher, and mystic Pythagorus who, despite his errant occult beliefs, is credited with identifying the mathematical ratios[1] on which the musical scale is based, stated that the New Song composed "the entire creation into melodious order."[2]

---

[1] This 'discovery' appears to have come out of a journey to Mesopotamia where he possibly adapted the knowledge of the ancient Semitic cultures.
[2] James, Jamie. *Music of the Spheres.* New York: Copernicus Springer-Verlag, 1995, p.69.

3

Inspiration: The Divine Process

The need to express the internal realities that define one's belief system is something that is fundamental to the human experience. It is this very need, in fact, that accounts for the artistic and religious expressions throughout history. This motivating factor has emboldened men even in the most dire of circumstances. It was the creative drive that caused Beethoven to persist in his work despite suffering the horrible malady of a nearly complete loss of hearing. While overcoming the temptation to commit suicide, he stated that it was *his art* that gave him the will to persist. A similar need for expression caused the prophets of the Bible and the apostles of Christ to lay down their lives for their religious faith. Countless others in history have chosen suffering and death rather than to deny their expressions of the heart. As James, the brother of Jesus tells us, "Faith without works (or expression) is dead" (James 2:20).

Responsible Delivery

On the converse of these examples stand many modern teachers and writers claiming to have a revelation from God. While some level of truth is normally necessary in order to attract an audience, a shocking lack of accountability and integrity in how one's views are presented is much in evidence today. It is the ability to carry a revelation without relying upon the *needless* tearing down of previously established truth that characterizes the responsible delivery of any new message. Those who are seeking an audience for themselves ought to consider the damage that ignorance of this principle may cause to their following as well as the ultimate accountability that they will have before the Lord. It is a difficult and laborious task to prove newly found truth and change long-held concepts, but one that is well worth the effort if done responsibly.

Beyond having a desire for being an expressive instrument, one must have training and fluency in the medium with which he is to work. In the case of the biblical prophets this would have included the study of Hebrew, which was the scholarly language of ancient Israel, and music (see chapter 6). Then in order to have one's work transmitted faithfully over time, a written tradition in the same areas is indicated. One must also have the humility to stay within his area of gifting and expertise, so as not to 'taint' the message that he wishes to transmit.

The 'Process'

Given these assertions, let us take a look at how the ancient prophets of the Bible may have received the scriptural inspiration they so effectively transmitted. We know that prayer and meditation, or quiet communion with God, was part of the daily life of the righteous men of old, "My soul waits for the LORD more than those who watch for the morning" (Ps.130:6, also see Ps. 27:7, 46:10, 62:5-8). As has been aptly stated, "without silence there is no music."[1] We also know that these men were literate in both the Hebrew language and ancient musical notation.

As early as the time of Moses there apparently existed a form of notation. (We see this command by the Almighty to "write down this song" to teach to Israel. [Deut. 31:19].) Songs by definition have specific melodies, and the inspired scripture supports our thesis. Therefore, while waiting upon the Lord, the prophets likely heard a still small voice (1Kings 19:12), in a song (Exod. 15:1) and proceeded to write both lyric and melody.[2]

Although the seasoned theologian may bristle at such a suggestion, apparently the Hebrew culture had established an expectation for receiving their prophetic revelations in song form. This would explain New Testament references (Rev 5:9, 14:3) as well as the early church's fondness for alluding to Christ as the New *Song*.

We are also told that the hand of the LORD comes upon the prophet when the strummer (instrumentalist) plays (2 Kings 3:14); thus a connection is made to instrumental music and prophecy. This process would not be foreign to

---

[1] Sherman, Russell. *Piano Pieces* New York. North Point Press, 1997. pg.130.
[2] See chapter 6 for more insight.

any songwriter in history except for the purity of the source and the profundity of the result. (Since writing on this I have begun to notice a pattern of inspirational thoughts, both musical and literary, coming from good 'practice' sessions.)

In light of the scriptural evidence provided, such a connection of music to prophecy should be an idea for serious consideration. To argue that the statement "the Lord is . . .my song" (Exod. 15:1) is merely allegorical is to risk also having to state that His being our "strength and salvation" is likewise allegory, something that no true theologian is likely to entertain. The evidence presented in this book, much of which has not before been suggested, when taken in sum, must lead one to the conclusion that this is at the least, a highly credible scenario.

We may also receive insight into the creative process from the realm of secular music. The aforementioned musical giant, Ludwig von Beethoven, claimed that he received his musical inspiration during promenades in the woods "in the *silence* of the night...when roused by moods", these thoughts then took musical shape for him.[1] It is doubtless that some form of solitude and introspection is fundamental for any composer or like creative mind.

The concept of inspiration is one that also indicates the involvement of a force that takes us outside the strong human predisposition towards habitual responses. There is some connection to an existing tradition and discipline that is a necessary precursor to inspired work. However, what defines the creative mind is the ability to incorporate what has gone before and to add to it in a relevant and often unexpected manner. These principles apply to the

---

[1] *Thayer' s Life of Beethoven*, rev. & ed., E. Forbes, Princeton, 1967, I, 304-06. (Grout p 516).

Inspiration: The Divine Process

revelation of scripture as well as to the progress of serious music throughout recorded history. Of course the word inspiration itself gives us a clue as to origin of profound ideas: inspire = *in spirit*.

An inspiration may come gradually, or sometimes "all at once." In either case, the working out of the inward idea into its expressive medium usually involves a *process*. In performance mediums the two elements, however, may coincide. This occurrence provides the ultimate experience for both artist and audience and is indeed the goal of all great performance. Jazz and classical improvisation is based on the ethos of spontaneous creativity in this context.

The receiving of a 'vision' is something that also characterizes inspired thought. Here a detailed scenario for the future comes to the individual in full form. A vision may or may not be fully understood at the time it is received, yet the clarity of the details are unmistakable. In the Bible, when a vision is given, an interpretation always follows. A vision is usually a larger plan that requires an extensive time period in which to work itself out. It may involve others who need to be brought in to the plan as well. In the case of the biblical prophets, their noteworthy visions typically involved those of future generations and the working out of a plan touching all mankind. The Bible is partial to this type of inspiration, for it states that, "Where there is no vision, the people parish" (Pr. 29:18a KJV).

As always, the level of inspiration for revelations that may come to one at anytime should always be 'checked' as to their source. This may be done by referring to the sacred texts, discussing ideas with trustworthy people in the faith, and the use of like practices. Oxford Group participants used 'four absolutes' as a standard for checking ideas. They checked to see if their inspirations lined up with standards embodied by the teachings of Christ, absolute 1) honesty 2) purity 3) selflessness and 4) love.

However the process of inspiration ultimately chooses to manifest within the individual, one thing is clear: musicians and poets have been observed to operate on a different level from others within their respective cultures. This was certainly no truer than with the inspired prophets of scripture.

Art or Athletics?

Different analogies are used in scripture to portray the spiritual life, including art, romance, sports, and battle. (Scripture also links music and battle together, as in 2Chron 20:21). But the balance has tipped way out of proportion in our sports-crazed society today. Sermons are replete with references to team sports and popular events such as the 'Super Bowl,' analogizing these events to principles for Christian living. It may be said that music and art, more so than competitive sports, have historically been the primary vehicle used to elucidate spiritual realities. The abundance of religious themes within great art and music throughout history poignantly testifies of this relationship.

Sporting events condition us to be competitive in life's pursuits. This ethic indeed dominates us today in business, politics, romance, and even spirituality. While having some positive influence, there exist dangers to an overly competitive orientation to life. Frank Buchman cautioned against relying upon a competitive approach in advancing the Christian faith, stating that one may, "win the argument, but lose their man." It seems that it would be more beneficial if believers could learn from the model of a symphony orchestra, which must work in *harmony*, and not in competition with each other, to produce their music. The desired result from such cooperation being an enjoyable art, not the mere conquest of the 'other team.'

There is another caution here for the church. The focus on competition and sports so prevalent in modern culture is directly traceable to the Greek culture. With their Olympic games came the glorification of human achievement. The ancient Greeks, then the Romans built great monuments to their sporting pursuits. It was then the sporting coliseums (i.e. football stadiums) of the Romans that facilitated the martyrdom of Christians, when it became the popular form of public entertainment.

By this I don't mean to suggest that people should not engage in competitive sports, rather to challenge the popular notion that they should be *paid*, and exorbitantly so, for such frivolous, and culturally questionable pursuits.

Music and Idol Worship

One notable ancient use of music is recorded in the book of Daniel. Here, music was used to direct the people of ancient Babylon to worship a false god, "that at the time you hear the sound of the horn, flute, harp, lyre, and psaltery, in symphony with all kinds of music, you shall fall down and worship the gold image that King Nebuchadnezzar has set up; and whoever does not fall down and worship shall be cast into the midst of a burning fiery furnace"(Dan.3:5-6).

In the modern context, one may identify his own idols by observing what is associated with the music that he listens to. Music characteristically accompanies such things as sporting events, all forms of advertisements for material goods (the golden image), endorsements of alcoholic beverages and drugs, promotion of occult ideologies, the glorifying of sex, and so on. As the king of Babylon represents in scriptural type the prophesied AntiChrist, one may also expect this end-time figure to use music prominently during his mad reign. In view of the previous list, much of modern music is already, in effect, tending toward such a use.

4
Musical Tonality: The Fingerprint of God

Historical and scriptural references indicate a greater role for music than is conventionally understood. Something unsuspected by scholars to date, is that music may be used as an interpretive 'key' to the prophecies of the Bible. The fundamental study of music theory reveals a template by which one may interpret the major dramas of the Bible, including the difficult prophecies of the end-times.

The ancient writers, Pythagorus, Plato, St. Augustine, as well as the biblical authors, all connected music to the Divine. They did not, however, all identify with the same God or gods. What follows is proof, based on tonal physics, which unmistakably identifies the God of the Bible as the source of the resultant musical art. It will simultaneously provide an interpretive key to the scriptures and prophecy, such as has been sought throughout recorded history.

Musical tonality is known historically to exist on the principle of *tension and release*. The various tones within the diatonic scale are not all equal; rather they play against each other as alternately complementary and antagonistic dramatic elements. This melodious playing out of a tonal drama is what 'moves' music, and therefore its listeners, forward. The same principle is at work in the dramas of the Bible. We also find a unity between the dramatic elements of musical tonality and those of the Bible and history. The same elements are at work, shaping their respective dramas, using the very same principles of tension and release, and in like manners. In this context, let us begin to examine these assertions.

Biblical Numerology and the Scale

In order to produce intelligible musical sound, composers throughout history have relied on the seven-tone scale. These major and minor sounding modes, not surprisingly, correspond to the biblical number for divine completion. The biblical sevens include; the days of Creation, the seven millennium of human history, the Crucifixion week of Christ, and the seven year Tribulation Period. Seven also defines the branches of the menorah and the number of biblical feasts. This number is no less foundational in music.

As we shall see, it is imperative for the interpreter of Bible prophecy to have a correct understanding of the dramatic structure of the biblical week. The musician must likewise gain a correct understanding of the tonal 'sevens' of the diatonic scale in order to master his art. These apparently unrelated disciplines also transfer from one to the other. Recall that the biblical prophets were also schooled in music (1Sam10:5).

As to music, the sense of the scale being *complete* by its use of seven-tone modes is proven out in practically every musical selection known to us today. Whether enjoying classical, jazz, popular, or even ancient music, it is to this seven-note structure that we owe our gratitude. Though variations exist, such as the pentatonic (5-tone) scale, and the diminished/ altered (8 +) scale, it is only with a careful respect for the physics of the underlying diatonic (7-tone) system that they are constructed.

The biblical number eight signifies *new beginnings*; as in circumcision (the eighth day), the Resurrection revealed, the Second Advent (the resolution to the Tribulation Week) and the New Heavens and New Earth (after the seventh millennium-the eighth day or Eternal State).

It is through the musical octave that the scale, too, is reborn into new registers, reaching to dizzying heights and awe-inspiring depths of tonal expression. We are allowed the pleasures of bass tones and kettle-drum sounds; also the cello, violin, clarinet, and flute due to this phenomenon of musical renewal at the octave. The differing registers then combine to give us rich textures and harmonies as well as delightful counter-melodies and variously pitched voices. The soprano, alto, tenor, and bass also owe their existence to the scale being reborn at the octave.

The next significant number is 'twelve.' Biblically, this is the number of divine government, or fullness. Twelve months govern both the solar and lunar calendars. Twelve tribes were the complete government, or zodiac of ancient Israel, and twelve apostles were chosen to bring the gospel of Christ to the world and to govern His first New Covenant church.

The number twelve 'governs' music also. In order to modulate to all the key centers, the twelve-tone or 'chromatic' scale is employed. This scale is found by counting the black and white piano keys within the octave. It is this scale that gives us the fullness by which a composition may be constructed. By applying the twelve tones of musical government, we are able to fully appreciate all the 'colors' and modulations of pitch. It is this system of twelve that allowed J.S. Bach to pen his masterpieces of counterpoint, not needing to stop to tune when desiring to change key or when borrowing notes from other modes or 'sevens.' We may also enjoy the richness of a Mozart, or Chopin or a good jazz performance because of this divine musical form of government. (If nothing else is accomplished here, hopefully the aspiring musician will be more enthusiastic in performing his or her scale exercises.)

Despite such compelling analogies, some will want to point to the anomalies of cultures that create 'microtonal' systems on which to base their music. These systems have either failed wholesale, creating only cacophonous noise (ask a proponent to 'hum' a tune that uses such a system), or they have merely been used to embellish an underlying diatonic (seven-tone) system. An example of the latter technique is seen in the melodies of Arabic music, as well as bended or slurred notes in western music. These, too, in order to be intelligible to their audience, must maintain the diatonic system as the underlying organizing structure.

The following chart lists the relevant biblical numerology and the corresponding Hebrew names of the scale degrees (ordered according to Haik-Vantoura). Notice the similarities in descriptive content.

Biblical Number/ Scale Degree	Ancient Hebrew Scale
1 Beginning, Source/ Tonic	1 *Silluq* (end) *origin*, completion
2 Testimony/ Supertonic	2 *Merkha* (prolonged) indecision
3 Perfect Testimony/ Mediant	3 *Tifha* (handbreadth) precision
4 Creation/ Subdominant	4 *Atnah* (rest) division, definition
5 Grace Atonement/ Dominant	5 *Munah* (set) suspension-resting
6 Man, earth/ Superdominant	6 *Darga* (step) foundation, deposition
7 Divine Completion/ Leading Tone	7 *Tevir* (broken) relaxation, evasion
8 New Beginnings/ Octave	Unlike western mode structures, the tonic is in the position of the third [67<u>1</u>2345] and resolves only to the tonic from below, *not to the octave.**
12 Divine Government/ Chromatic Scale	Modulations or non-scale tones are not used in the ancient biblical music.

* The significance of this structure is shown at the conclusion of chapter six.

"It's about the melody"

Other cultures, more primitive and deeply attached to pagan concepts of divinity, rely on repetitious rhythmic motifs as a basis for their music. Whereas rhythm as a complementary element to existing melodic and harmonic structures is evident in great music throughout history, it is the relative lack of the latter elements and the simplicity and redundancy of the former that characterize the more primitive forms. Contemporary pop culture has now degraded to such a base level in the use of 'rap,' 'trance,' and even the root traditions themselves (i.e. 'native drumming'). In the dumbing-down process that has taken us from classical music to pop/rock music, it is this use of repetitious rhythmic devices and simplistic melodic formulas that ultimately define the latter.

In this context we should note that *melody*, not rhythm and harmony, has long been regarded as the 'heart' of the musical composition, whether classical or popular. Great music, it has been observed, has great melodies. Although great composers are known for making advances with various elements such as rhythm, harmony, form, and meter, they have fundamentally been great melodists. Our tendency to recall a composer's work primarily by its melodic contours attests to this reality.

As this 'civilizing' melodic element (the 'heart' of music) has been progressively removed from much of today's musical life, one must begin to ask if this doesn't reflect or even help to create a people lacking the same attribute, heart.

Further corroboration of the principle of melodic importance is seen in a phenomenon known as the "Mozart effect." Behavioral scientists have observed that the playing of the recordings of Mozart to infants and small children brings about an increase in intelligence indicators. As perhaps history's greatest composer, Mozart wrote music that is above all, *highly melodic*. And he used rhythm as a complement to his great melodies in a subtle and non-intrusive manner, something characteristic of most of the great composers. This principle may serve as a guide for the modern listener who wishes to deliver himself from the bombast that is in much of today's popular music.

Another trend today is the attempt to identify 'sacred' vibrations, based on mystical mathematical formulas, which supposedly bring some sense of healing or power to the individual. This notion is gaining some popularity in recent times. Here again we need look for truth and balance.

Occult religions have long practiced the chanting of sacred mantras, such as 'o-o-hm,' for the purpose of inducing an altered mental state in their followers. Musically speaking, such practices are but exercises in extreme 'boredom,' yet spiritually they may be hypnotic and therefore dangerous. Any healing to be found in music, as we saw from the example of David and king Saul, comes from being exposed to the work of a skilled or gifted artisan, filled with the spirit of God, not from a single 'sacred' chant, mode, or scientific formula.

In the context of serious music, it was the composers of the twentieth-century that ultimately succeeded in breaking down the system of tonality that has carried music throughout history. Arnold Schoenberg and his 'twelve-tone' disciples achieved this ultimate departure from anything heartfelt in the domain of serious music. Rather than a melody that connected to human emotions with heartfelt expressions, Schoenberg's are based only on mathematical formulas, specifically aimed at breaking-down the intrinsic system of tension and release within the musical scale. The music that is produced from the twelve-tone approach is, to say the least, not very 'hum-able.' This twentieth century development also represented, by way of musical symbolism, the ultimate musical departure from Christ and the Bible. The truth of this statement will continue to prove itself out as we now begin an examination of the symbolism of the scale itself.

The Scale: A Prophetic 'Meta-Type'

"I have also spoken by the prophets, and have multiplied visions; I have given symbols through the witness of the prophets." (Hos.12:10)

As has been demonstrated, the intervals created within the tonal scale have direct correlations to the 'days' of the biblical weeks. Musical intervals are determined by counting number of scale degrees from one pitch to the next. The intervals found within the diatonic octave or seven-note scale also have their application to the correct interpretation of the prophetic scriptures.

God had always intended His prophetic revelations to be understood by way of applicable *keys* of understanding. Speaking to the prophet Hosea, He declares this reality (Hosea 12:10). He also has declared the end from the beginning (Is.41:26), in that historical events repeat themselves in *type*. Such keys are necessary to the *correct* interpretation of Bible prophecy. This truth is reinforced by the many errant attempts at prophetic interpretations made without the respect for this principle. The proliferation of such failures is no more evident than in our time.

Here is where, again, music comes to the rescue. We know from observations made throughout history that music is a precise *symbolic* language, capable of accurately conveying dramatic meaning to its listeners. The opening motif of Beethoven's Fifth Symphony, or Handel's Hallelluja chorus are but two of the countless examples of this powerful expressive ability within music.

Through the skillful use of melody, harmony, and rhythm, the musical composer is able to take his audience from the depths of despair, to heights of untold elation. Something previously unsuspected however, is that musical tonality is itself a *key* to understanding the prophetic scriptures, and a precise and wondrous one at that.

This also represents the first time that just such an extra-biblical phenomenon has been documented to be a true interpretive key to the Bible. I have coined the word *meta*-type, meaning *transcendent*, to convey that this 'type' also works on multiple levels.

The scale 'meta-type'
Twelve-tone scale (black and white notes)

-Tri-tone-
(mid-point)

Tonic 2nd 3rd 4th 5th 6th 7th Octave
      S-T M SubD Dom S-D L-T

Theoreticians throughout history, have observed and identified the qualities within the physics of the tonal scale, that make music function as 'audible drama.' Something that they have missed, however, is that the character of the various tones of the scale find their counterparts in the major dramas of the Bible: The seven days of Creation, the seven thousand year 'week' of human history, the Crucifixion Week of Christ, and the sevens of the Apocalypse (the seals and trumpets specifically). [1]

We shall now overview the scale degrees and their respective biblical counterparts. In music theory, the alterations of pitch that help determine modality, e.g., major, minor, diminished, are not particularly relevant to the *function* of the scale degree within the given mode. Whether major or minor, the third scale degree, for example, has a particular function within the scale. The *function* of the scale degree is what will primarily be addressed, and not the various modalities that are possible. (The striking characteristics of the non-scale tritone [aug. 4th] will be noted, however.)

The Tonic or First Degree

This is the primary point of rest within the musical scale, whether in the major or minor modes. Compositions throughout history characteristically begin and end on this degree of the scale. This tone defines the musical center of any given piece. The first day of the week within scripture has a like function. The first day defines the basic center of the narrative, i.e., it *sets the tone*. The first day of Creation,

---

[1] Parallels within the biblical weeks were notably documented by Tim Cohen in the manuscript *Messiah, History, and the Tribulation Period*, (Prophecy House, Aurora, CO. 1994, not yet published.) Though mistakenly termed, 'harmonies,' they are more literally, 'unisons.'

God created *the heavens and the earth*. He also created light and separated night and day. These events define the center or the setting for the rest of the events of the drama of history and the scriptures. The first millennium of history likewise sets up the human drama to follow as well as its main characters, as laid out in the first chapters of Genesis. The first day of the Crucifixion Week has Christ entering Jerusalem with cries of "Peace in Heaven and Glory in the Highest" (Luke 19:38b), thus stating the principle theme and focus of the week's events, i.e., spiritual peace with God. The first year of the Tribulation Week begins with a peace treaty with Israel, thus setting the stage and focus for that week's events (Dan. 9:27). Here the focus returns to national Israel and a process that culminates with millennial peace and the Messiah's reigning from Mt. Zion. All are beginning themes to which the stories return as their respective sevens play out and resolve.

The Second, Third and Fourth

The intermediary scale degrees have their respective correlations to the Bible as well. The second, third, and fourth help define and carry the drama to the more striking events found in the other intervals (and their biblical counterparts). In the case of the first two, "flavor" may be added to a composition by using them in their major or minor forms.

The second scale degree challenges the status quo of the tonic, creating a conflict of sound between the two. The third, as does its biblical counterpart, gives 'perfect testimony' as to modality (major or minor). Here, in the biblical context, the drama is also further defined. The fourth, or 'sub-dominant' helps bring us to the striking events of the tritone (augmented fourth) and dominant fifth.

The Tritone or 'Blue-Note'

A striking correlation is found with the interval of the tri-tone. By counting three and one-half steps into the scale, we come to a highly *dissonant* interval. This sound is typically used for sirens, trains, and the like. It creates the most possible tension within the context of the musical scale and is the most in need of a release or resolution in order to maintain a harmonious composition. When used in modern music it is called the "blue-note" because of its ability to produce a mournful quality within the scale. Classical musicians of the 1940's referred to the tri-tone as *intervale al diavlo* or devil's interval,[1] as it was the primary tonal device within the jazz and be-bop movement. This is a most telling description in view of its biblical counterparts; the Babylonian captivity, the arrest and trial of Christ, and the start of the Great Tribulation. This interval also symbolically helped to express the struggles of American blacks as well as to define a related musical style, i.e. jazz and blues. The blue-note is also the exact *mid-point* of the octave.

As mentioned, the blue-note has a direct counterpart in the biblical weeks. It was three and one-half millennium into biblical history when the nation of Israel experienced extreme discord as it (sadly) went into the Babylonian captivity. Likewise, a close study of the gospels reveals that it was *mid-week* when the betrayal and arrest of Christ occurred. (This presupposes a study that many have yet to undertake, that of a fourth-day crucifixion and seventh-day resurrection of the Messiah (see following section). Not only does this view better harmonize the gospel accounts,

---

[1] Ken Burns *Jazz*. P.B.S. Denver, CO Jan. 29-31.

(the only approach, in fact, that does), and provide for a literal interpretation of the prophecies (the three days and three nights in the tomb as a 72 hour period (Matt. 12:40), but it also aligns the Crucifixion Week with the other 'sevens' of the Bible and the musical scale.)

What is termed the Great Tribulation for the Church and Israel at the culmination of history occurs three and one-half years into the Tribulation Week. These events include a desecration of the Jewish alter, the beginning of the persecution of the church, and the Tribulational capture of Israel (Rev. 11:1-3, Rev. 13:1-2, Mic. 4:9-11). Thus, the major dissonant biblical events occur at the exact mid-point of their respective 'sevens,' thereby correlating to, and playing in unison with, the tri-tone (devil's interval) within our musical scale.

The Fifth or 'Dominant'

The most prominent interval in the biblical context is that of the trumpet call, or the rising fifth interval. It is known as the 'pure' or perfect interval of the scale (along with the sub-dominant fourth and the octave), indicating a lack of modulation in pitch when the notes sound together. This interval is naturally produced when air pressure is increased into a brass instrument or a ram's horn. It is also a primary 'overtone' produced by a vibrating instrument string.

The musical device of the fifth interval, or trumpet call, is used in the biblical context at the start of the feasts, at the New Moons (beginning of the month), for battles, to warn of impending judgment, for weddings, and coronations. The interval, played to standing ovations in many religious assemblies today, has an awakening or attention getting effect on its hearers. It is therefore quite natural that it be an introduction to important biblical festivities and events.

Interestingly, the Jewish biblical feast Rosh Hashanah or the "Feast of Trumpets," is thought by many Rabbis to have been the birth date of Adam. As a close study of the Gospels reveals, the birth of Christ was of necessity in the fall, (not the winter as church tradition teaches), and almost certainly coincided with one of the fall feasts, and certainly not a pagan holiday (such as Christmas, the 'winter solstice').

In this author's opinion, Rosh HaShanah is the most likely candidate for Christ's birth. Christ, the 'second Adam,' would not only share His incarnate birth date with the first Adam, but also the feast named after the musical event that identifies Him throughout scripture (the trumpet call), and the one that begins the civil year within Judaism.

In analyzing the music from the Hebrew Creation account (see Appendix I), I was encouraged to find the fifth interval used consistently to announce the Word of the Lord ("and God said"). Notice also that in the Apocalypse the seventh trumpet *sounds* for a period of days announcing the coming of the Word, Jesus the Messiah, back to the earth (Rev. 10:7). The same trumpet also announces the beginning of the Millennial Kingdom (Rev. 11:15).

Two types of trumpet blasts are used within Jewish tradition at the start of the biblical feasts. These carry an interesting symbolism as well. One type of blast is the *teruah*. This is characteristically the rising fifth interval, accenting the fifth tone. Five is symbolic of purity and Divinity. The other blast is a repeated staccato tone, at the fifth, called *tekiah*. The Hebrew word means "to drive a stake," as in execution. This ancient Jewish musical tradition therefore poignantly dramatizes the sacrifice of

Christ, who is God (*teruah*), and was nailed to a tree (*tekiah*) in His crucifixion.

Also, the *sounding* of the seventh trumpet from heaven (for a number of days) is the only way biblically to identify the start of the Millennial Kingdom (Rev.11:15). The Greek word *salpizo* is used to describe this event and translates "to sound a blast," or "to trumpet." Thus it is that we will have a *literal musical cue* with which to mark the start of this great event. (It has been suggested by some that this will be fulfilled as air-raid sirens sound worldwide [also the fifth interval] to call the armies of the nations to battle against Christ as He is seen approaching the earth.)

Some have attempted to predict the start of the Messianic period by supposedly restoring a correct biblical calendar. The authors claim to have identified the beginning of the year 6,000 (the seventh millennium of history) by blending astronomical data with biblical accounts of historical events. Predictions have been offered for specific dates of prophesied events such as war and economic collapse based on these calculations. Although several of the dates have already proven to be false, people seem riveted to the notion that they can know of the Messianic era ahead of time based on such information.

(Our Gregorian calendar is dated from an arbitrary reckoning of Christ's birth approximately two thousand years ago, and is somewhat misleading as to where we are in biblical history (missing 4,000 or so years). The Jewish calendar, showing the year as 5762, is also inaccurate, missing some 240 years in its reckoning of time due to the fourth century omissions of Hillel II and mistakes in calculations from the book of Numbers).

As is documented in the section 'Date-Setters and Prophetic Truth' (chapter 9), such a claim does not square with Bible prophecies which indicate that a corrected calendar will not be in place for such specific date calculations *prior* to the Tribulation period, (notwithstanding the many sincere efforts to produce one).

The fifth interval also harmonizes with the fifth day in the Bible. As its tonal nature is *harmonic purity* and as it is a *point of rest* within the scale, we see a spiritual counterpart in the fifth seal of the Apocalypse, where the martyred saints are given white robes *(purity)* and told to *rest* for a short time (intermediate) (Rev. 6:9-11). During the Crucifixion Week, Christ *rested* in the earth after He had *purified* the world of sin with His shed blood. In the fifth millennium, the people of the earth were offered rest, as the atonement (purity) for sin was accomplished through Christ at the end of the fourth millennium.

Not only does the study of this divine interval serve to authenticate the interpretive system that I used for the music of Genesis (see Chapter 5), but it also demonstrates the sovereign command that the biblical Author had over all the elements and symbolism of His narration, cover to cover.

The Sixth or 'Superdominant'

The sixth day in scripture thematically speaks of *dominion of the earth*. In the Creation week God gave Adam earthly dominion on this day. In the sixth millennium of history (approximately 1000-2000 C.E.), man *dominates* the earth by greatly increasing in population and technology until the sixth trumpet of the sixth seal of the Apocalypse when God begins to reassert His earthly dominion. Earthly dominion also proceeds from heavenly dominion (the fifth).

The AntiChrist, who *dominates* the earth for the last three and one half years of human history is associated with the number 666 (600+60+6). The western musicologists aptly named the sixth-scale degree the super*dominant*, however without understanding its biblical/prophetic counterpart. Matching to its numerology, this interval of the *sixth* (earthly dominion) follows the dominant *fifth* (heavenly dominion), and it functions to add color and drama to the musical scale.

In western tonality the sixth is the major scale degree on which the minor scale is begun. The minor scale is also known to produce a sad and mournful quality. This also matches the theme of man's dominion and, of course, that of the AntiChrist. The musicologists, therefore, in responding honestly to the musical realities of our harmonic system were also describing the imagery of the sixth day in the biblical drama with an eerie accuracy.

The Seventh or 'Leading-Tone'

The 'leading tone' or interval of the seventh has a profound biblical correlation. This interval is somewhat dissonant in nature and as its name suggests, demands a resolution, by nature to the octave. As part of the dominant fifth chord, it is also a point of rest (sabbath). Of course the weekly sabbath is on the seventh day also and has a theme of resting from labor, but less well known, a secondary theme of tension.

The sevens in a scriptural context have a kind of built-in tension that may be seen as propellant into their respective eights. The seventh day of the Crucifixion Week found the apostles and followers of Jesus tense over whether the resurrection had occurred. It was only upon going to the tomb at the start of the week, they learned the news of the resurrection (resolution). "Now on the first day of the week, very early in the morning, they . . . came to the tomb . . . But they found the stone rolled away" (Luke 24:1-2). (Discrepancies exist in the wording of the other gospel accounts of the Resurrection (indicating Sunday rather than late Saturday). These are due variously to a mistranslation from the Greek text, and misplaced punctuation in the English text. See following section for more details.)

The Tribulation Week for the church and Israel culminates with the eventful judgments (seven trumpets) of the seventh seal (year), and likewise resolve with the return of Christ at what would be the eighth year and the start of the Millenial Reign. (Rev. 11:15).

The week of history is likewise parallel. It is at the end of the millennial kingdom (seventh day of the week of history) that the final Satan-lead rebellion against Christ occurs, thus creating a final tension and 'leading to' the Eternal State (eight day).

The seventh also denotes completion of the scale as the Sabbath does the biblical week.

The Octave and the Eighth Day

The musical scale is reborn as well as elevated as the seven-note scale resolves to the octave. With this resolution the musical scale comes to a point of final rest, with the tonic being now *elevated*. This theme plays out within the weeks of scripture. As previously mentioned, the number eight is that of 'new beginnings' in scripture.

The week of human history resolves when the seventh millennium (Messianic Reign) gives way to the Eternal State (eighth millennium). The Crucifixion Week resolves as the seventh day resurrection of Christ and the saints is revealed on the eighth day (Matt 27:53). The Tribulation Week resolves as the seventh year comes to an end and the eighth year ushers in the Sabbath Millennium (Rev. 11:15).

Each biblical week carries a sense of final resolution to its drama and an elevation from its previous state (tonic), restating each initial theme, although in a 'higher' register (from the tonic to the octave). The Old Heavens and Earth become the New Heavens and New Earth, the Triumphal Entry into Jerusalem becomes the triumph over death and hell (Resurrection Revealed), and the false peace of the AntiChrist becomes the true peace of Christ in the Millenial Reign. Life imitating art, to coin a cliché.

A crowning corroboration of the scale 'meta-type' is found in biblical numerology. The ancient Greeks and Hebrews, and thus the early church, calculated the numerical value of words utilizing an inspired system of gematria. The New Testament references this practice in relation to the name value of the AntiChrist (Rev. 13:18). In this system, the letters of a given word have a numerical significance, which may be added together. The sum values may then be calculated to reveal hidden meanings. Jesus' name in Greek, Ιησους (10+8+200+70+400 +200), adds up to eight hundred and eighty-eight using this ancient system. A number that is given with its 'tenth' and its 'hundredth,' in biblical numerology, becomes the 'ultimate' expression of what the number symbolizes. The Anti-Christ (666), is the *ultimate* earthly man, as six is the number of man. The number eight we know to represent 'elevation' and 'new beginnings.' Jesus, by the calculation of his name, is then the *ultimate elevated* man (888).

Here then is the supreme spiritual ascension for all mankind, and the ultimate resolution 'to the octave.' It is also further proof that indeed "All things were made through Him, and without Him nothing was made that was made." (John 1:3). Certainly we may now know that this scripture is fulfilled in terms of the sublime gift of music.

The Greek Alphabet and Gematria

Α α	Β β	Γ γ	Δ δ	Ε ε	Ζ ζ	Η η	Θ θ
1	2	3	4	5	7	8	9
Ι ι	Κ κ	Λ λ	Μ μ	Ν ν	Ξ ξ	Ο ο	Π π
10	20	30	40	50	60	70	80
Ρ ρ	Σ σς	Τ τ	Υ υ	Φ φ	Χ χ	Ψ ψ	Ω ω
100	200	300	400	500	600	700	800

(This chart is parallel to the ancient Hebrew gematria)

The 4th day Crucifixion, 7th day Resurrection of Christ and the Musical scale

Companion to this study is the proper interpretation of the events of the Crucifixion Week of Christ. Christian tradition teaches a Friday crucifixion (late on the 6th day) and Sunday resurrection (early on the 8th day). This view presents basic problems with the gospel accounts. What follows is a brief overview of a somewhat complex study.

Firstly, Christ stated He would be in the tomb three days and three nights, or 72 hours (Matt. 12:40). The Friday evening to Sunday morning rendering allows for no more than 36 hours, and therefore presents a conflict.

Second, the gospel accounts, when cross-referenced, indicate that the apostles observed two sabbath days after the crucifixion and one day to labor before the resurrection. This would make the sabbath after the crucifixion a Thursday Passover Sabbath, not the Saturday rest that most Gentile interpreters suppose (Mk. 15:42). The intermediate day of activity would have been Friday (the preparation for the weekly sabbath), and Saturday the *second* sabbath of that week. At the end of this day the resurrection then occurs in fulfillment of the "sign of Jonah" (Matt.12:40), a literal 72-hour period. His resurrection was then *revealed* on Sunday (feast of First Fruits).

Superficial anomalies exist in the English text with regard to this day in two of the gospels. These may be accounted for by observing translation and punctuation errors in the English text. Matthew 28:1, when correctly translated from the Greek, clearly states that the two Mary's went to the tomb late on the weekly sabbath when they found the empty tomb, not early on Sunday. "The first phrase *opse . . . sabbaton*, more naturally means "late on the Sabbath", while the verb *epiphosko*, translated [as] towards the dawn, is used in Luke 23:54 for the 'beginning' of a Jewish day in the evening."[1] The parallel scripture, Mark 16:9, agrees when properly punctuated: "Now when He rose, early on the first of the week he appeared to Mary the Magdalene . . ." (The comma is only placed after the word 'week' to support the Sunday resurrection theory.)[2] These gospel accounts then harmonize with the clear readings of Luke 24:1 and John 20:1.

The Hebrew name for the seventh scale degree, used in the prophetic book of the Psalms, also corroborates the 'seventh day' view of the resurrection. *Galgal*, which literally means "skull" or "rolling," is the Hebrew root word for the place of Christ's crucifixion, *Golgotha*, or 'the place of the skull' (and as Dr. Ernest L. Martin postulates, likely His nearby tomb).[3] We know that the stone that covered Christ's grave had been "rolled away" by an angel

---

[1] France, "Matthew," *Tyndale New Testament Commentaries*, No. 1 (Michigan: Eerdmans Publishing Company, 1985) p. 406.
[2] Cohen, Tim. *Messiah, History, and the Tribulation*. Prophecy House, Aurora, CO. 1994.
[3] Martin, Ernest L. *Secrets of Golgotha*. Oregon: Associates for Scriptural Knowledge, 1996, p.281.

to reveal His resurrection to the two women (Matt. 28:2). The seventh scale degree, its ancient Hebrew name, and the possible place of the resurrection, all harmonize with the gospel accounts as well as the imagery of the angel 'rolling away' the stone at the end of the seventh day of the week.

When taking into account all the symbolism within the musical scale, in particular the tri-tone (for the crucifixion), and the Hebrew name of the seventh scale degree (*galgal*), we see that a better understanding of music helps to settle the intensely debated theological issue as to the true timing of the events within the Crucifixion Week of Christ, a surprising validation of the importance of music within the realm of biblical scholarship.

The Scale and the Scriptural Weeks

Thus the function and character of the scale degrees of seven-note scales or modes (on which music throughout history is based) as identified by the music theorists correlate with the themes and character of their respective days of the week throughout the scriptures, history, and the Genesis Creation days. Tonal music has symbolically played the themes of the Bible (the Creation, Crucifixion, Tribulation weeks) and history, since the beginning of time. This relationship is not imaginary but real, profound, and undeniable when one sufficiently reviews the evidence. What follows is a sample of this phenomenon. See also, the Trumpet Judgments (Chapter 9), the Biblical Fugue (Appendix III).

Musical Tonality: The Fingerprint of God

Crucifixion Week	**Tribulation Week**
\multicolumn{2}{c}{**1st –Tonic**}	

1st –Tonic
Defines tonal center of piece, point of rest.

| Sun. - Day 1 Triumphal Entry, "peace in Heaven" (Jn12:12-13) | 1st Seal Peace treaty with Israel and AntiChrist (Rev 6:1) |

2nd -Supertonic
Adds "color", dramatic status quo is challenged

| Mon. - Day 2 Jesus' authority questioned (Mk11:19) Judas given author. to take Prince of Peace. | 2nd Seal Authority given, sword, to take away peace from earth (Rev 6:3) |

3rd -Mediant
Helps define "mode" (mood)

| Tues. - Day 3 Judas *paid* for betrayal of Christ. Lord & disciples on Mt.of Olives (place of crucifixion)[1] Matt 26:15 | 3rd Seal Scales (law of AntiChrist set up), monetary inflation (Rev 6:5). |

4th -Subdominant
Tritone, 'Blue-note', tension, dissonance

| Wed. - Day 4 Arrest, Trial, Crucifixion of Christ (Matt 26:50, 27:1, 27:33). | 4th Seal Great Trib. Israel and Church tried and persecuted (Rev 6:7-8). |

5th -Dominant
Purity, intermediate rest Dominion of Heaven

| Thurs. - Day 5 Christ put in earth (*rest*) sins of earth purged (in heaven) (Matt 27:62) | 5th Seal Martyrs *rest* (intermediate) in Heaven and are pure (Rev 6:9-11). |

---

[1] Dr. Ernest Martin asserts that Christ was likely crucified on the Mount of Olives as in accordance with early church tradition, not the post-Constantine (Temple of Venus) modern location. Martin, Ernest L. *Secrets of Golgotha*. Oregon: Associates for Scriptural Knowledge, 1996, p 250.

	6ᵗʰ -Superdominant
	Earthly Dominion
Fri. Day 6	6ᵗʰ Seal
Christ descends, takes dominion over death and hell. Apostles *prepare* for sabbath day. (Mark 16:1)	144K Sealed, God begins earthly dominion. Earth *prepared* for Sabbath Mill. (Rev 7:3)
	7ᵗʰ -Leading-tone
	Anticipation (rest as part of dominant chord)
Sat. - Day 7	7ᵗʰ Seal
Apostles rest, yet are tense not knowing outcome of Crucifixion Week. Resurrection at end of day (Matt. 28:6)	Preparation for Sabbath Mil. Tpt. judgments begin. Rapture at end of Tribulation Week (Rev. 8:2).
	Octave-final resolution
	Tonic restated in higher register
Sun. - Day 8	2ⁿᵈ Advent
Resurrection Revealed Resolution of Crucifixion Week (John 3:36).	Millennial Reign - Final resolution to Tribulation Week (Rev. 20:4).

Summary

Thus it is that music indeed plays the themes of God. In fact the entire Bible, the Creation, and importantly for this generation, the Apocalypse are carefully patterned in unison with the musical scale itself. The Composer of the Universe used the elements of the seven-tone musical scale in fashioning His drama, just as mortal composers throughout history have in fashioning their compositions. Conversely, it may be said that *every musical composition since the beginning of time*, in its use of musical tonality, *has played the great themes of Creation and the Bible* by weaving their tapestries from the Divine fabric of the musical scale.

5

The Musical Priesthood

On that day I will raise up the tabernacle of David, which has fallen down, and repair its damages; I will raise up its ruins, and rebuild it as in the days of old. Amos 9:11

To further our understanding of God's plan for the musical art, we need to consider the specific type (*tupos*) or pattern that He has laid out for us in scripture as it relates to music. As we shall see, music has been a central part of the Divine Order since the beginning, has experienced the Fall, the Redemption, and will be prominent in the Millennial Reign and the Eternal State.

The Fall

The first direct chronological reference to the musical art centers on Lucifer, the covering cherub in the original heavenly order (Ezek. 28:12-14). This heavenly worship leader was created with instruments of praise; timbrels, pipes, and stringed instruments as an integral part of his body (Isa. 14:11).

Contrary to popular myth, it was not because of the musical gift that this angelic being fell, but rather because his heart was lifted up by "abundance of trading" (merchandise) and his "beauty" (pride) (Ezek.28:16-17). The false god of the Bible, who was the chief musician prior to his fall, has empowered many to success in the arts and music throughout history. We must be mindful that he only has the power to corrupt use of a given talent. The talent itself is from God the Creator for "every good and perfect gift is from above" (James 1:17).

Someone who possesses a spiritual gifting is distinct from one who has been 'anointed', receiving a spiritual blessing on his or her work. There are many *gifted* artists today who are not dedicated to God in their work and therefore are not divinely anointed. In fact, it is apparent in many cases that their empowering is from quite another source. God will only bless that which is consecrated to His service. Of course, that Godly use is truly the highest application of any talent.

Next we are told of a person named *Jubal*, the "father of all who play harp and flute" (Gen.4:21). This seemingly innocuous reference in scripture, however, needs to be taken within its context. *Jubal*, from the corrupt lineage of Cain and living in the pre-flood era, was likely of the same ilk as the post-flood Nimrod, the king of Babylon. Although the Bible only describes Nimrod as a "mighty hunter," we know from context that he was much more. He is, in fact the primary figurehead for all the corrupted societies throughout the Bible.

Similarly, we may place *Jubal* as not just a prototypical music teacher, but as one who taught the rebellious nations of the pre-flood earth a corrupt usage of the art—the prototypical rock musician, if you will.

(Rock has appropriately been called the "music of rebellion" by modern cultural observers. While largely expressing the sentiments of the adolescent experience, pop/rock music conveys that time in life that is the most rebellious and disobedient in individual development. It is also the dominant form of musical style both inside and outside the church today.)

Clement of Alexandria likened *Jubal* and the pagan music of Orpheus (Thracian music), distinguishing between it and that of David, which served the higher "fatherly purpose of God."[1] This distinction was apparently assumed knowledge amongst the early church, as there was no further elaboration on the point.

The first post-flood reference to music was in Laban's interview with future son-in-law Jacob. Here, a celebratory use of music within a prosperous culture is referenced, "for I might have sent you away with joy and songs, with timbrel and harp" (Gen. 31:27b). We thus see that music was at the heart of the life of society even at that early time.

The Redemption

Next, we find the first 'God-ordained', redemptive use of music commanded to the patriarch Joseph, while he was yet in Egypt (Ps. 81:2-6). It was through the nation of Israel

---

[1] James, Jamie. *Music of the Spheres.* New York: Copernicus Springer-Verlag, 1995, p.70.

that God chose to work out His redemptive plan for mankind in general, and the musical art was a first priority. The features of this ordinance are quite striking.

While yet in Egypt, Joseph was given a statute and a law (v.4) for a complete liturgy of musical expression representing all major instrument groups (vv.2-3) to serve as a *testimony* to the nations (v.5). The Psalm goes on to describe that in turning from this command, the people of Israel experienced a curse instead of a blessing. What a weighty matter we are dealing with when we consider the Lord's plan for this art.

We next see the mention of a national song for Israel (Exod.15:1) and the Song of the Red Sea. After their deliverance from the land of Egypt and the bondage to Pharaoh, *b'nai* Israel spontaneously broke into song over the event (see Rev.15:2-3 as an end-time fulfillment). Among other things, this would presuppose that a common musical syntax already existed within the tribe. The narrative goes on to describe the use of rhythmic dance (with timbrels) to add to this expression of joy (Ex. 15:20-21).

Having established this early musical presence in Israel's spiritual life, not only described in the scriptures, but also noted melodically (in the Masoretic text, discussed in chapter 6), we may now move on to the direct specifications that were given to the nation for their musical worship.

The Torah, in describing the functions of the priesthood, mentions two main duties—that of the sacrificial atonement, and that of worship. Additionally the Priests were charged with general Temple maintenance. In each instance, it was *specialists* who were called upon to perform the duties. The qualifications, expectations, and rewards are all specifically laid out.

The first appointment is strictly lineal from that of Aaron, brother to Moses. As God chose Israel from among the nations, so He chose Aaron and his sons from amongst Israel. Others were chosen from among the lineage of the righteous who had proven their fidelity to the Lord (Exod. 32:26).

The sons of Levi, after Israel's general apostasy at Sinai, were the first to return and restore the Lord's order in the camp. For this they were entrusted with keeping the things of God, supplanting the position of the firstborn Reuben. The Hebrew word Levi means literally "my heart." As this was the tribe entrusted with the musical worship, could God's view on this art be made any clearer?

Later appointments were made through David, notably Asaph to conduct worship, with the former lineages being maintained. The Aaronic lineage was awarded the "most holy" work of the ministry.

The qualifications for all these appointments involve *skill, knowledge, and willingness* (1Chron. 15:22). It was not enough just to have a desire to be of service; one must also have had evidence of fitness for that post—what we call talent. Conversely, talent without knowledge and direction is a sure recipe for disaster. In addition to this, we see that the priests and worshipers alike were *wholehearted* in their musical expressions (1Chron 13:8).

While one can shirk at any one of these descriptions and even think of examples where embarrassing displays have been made in respect to recreating such scenarios today, we must rather see the totality of the picture here. Wholeheartedness without skill is pretense. Skill without passion is technical frigidity and aloofness. All such virtues existing apart from submission to God are "vanity and grasping for the wind" (Eccl. 2:11). It is the best of all qualities in right proportion, therefore, that is the mark, and a goal to strive for in ever increasing measure.

The musical priesthood was also hierarchical, from the Master of the Song (*Chenaniah*), to the Chief musicians and singers, to the 2nd degree musicians and singers (1Chron. 15:16-18). The need for order with submission to the greater artisans is in evidence just as it must be in any band or symphony orchestra throughout history. The conductor is the most skilled musician of the group, then section leaders, then ensembles. Without one or several leading and directing, musical and political anarchy is certain.

Qualifications/Procedures

Having chosen the musical priesthood for His people, God then introduces the orders for carrying out His ministrations.

First, the Levites were brought before the assembly and had hands laid upon them. This was done to denote their elevation to a place of distinction, and of service. It is here that the nation demonstrated its esteem for the office of the priesthood.[1] They then were set apart as a 'wave offering', a firstborn amongst Israel, and were brought before the Lord. Atoning sacrifices were made to cleanse them for their work. Having been purified, they washed their clothes; and then they began their apprenticeship and service. The principles entailed are appointment, sanctification (separation and elevation), purity and service.

An observation with regard to Temple purity that has escaped modern notice, is that the priests by law came up to

---

[1] Stone's Chumash, mesorah Publications, Ltd. Brooklyn, 1993. p. 777.

Jerusalem properly *trimmed*, washed, and attired.[1] This practice was to be imitated by the general population of Israel, as the priests were the models for all Israelite men. Consider, in this light, the subject of our modern image of Christ Himself. Most popular renderings since the fourth century have depicted Him with long rather than trimmed hair. Yet the gospels show Him teaching within the courts of the Temple (Matt.26:55), an event that would have been impossible under Jewish law had He not had "well-trimmed" hair.

Epiphanius of Salamis in A.D. 379-395 tried to alert believers to an alarming trend, of the circulating of pictures of a longhaired and bearded Christ. He pointed out the fallacies of depicting Him this way, thinking that He was a *Nazarite*.[2] The mere fact that Christ drank wine negates His being under this specific Old Testament vow. It was, in fact, the Greek philosophers and pagan deities of the time that were adorned with long hair, and not Jewish men—and certainly not the model Priest of all time! Jesus was, however, from the town of Nazareth and therefore rightly called a *Nazarene*. Perhaps this is how this confusion began.

Bishop Eusebius (of the Jerusalem church), in writing to Constantia, the sister of Emperor Constantine, warned that the use of any pictures depicting Christ in the flesh was a violation of the commandments and should be forbidden amongst Christians.[3] Those today who believe by wearing long hair that they are imitating Christ, or who keep the popular portraits depicting the Lord as wearing such, might

---

[1] Eidersheim, Alfred. *The Temple*. Mass: Hendrickson Publishers, Inc. 1994, p 62.
[2] Martin, Ernest L. *Secrets of Golgotha*. Oregon: Associates for Scriptural Knowledge, 1996, p.353.
[3] Ibid, p. 352.

do well to consider this history and to study the issue in an effort to be biblically correct. "Does not even nature itself teach you that if a man has long hair, it is a dishonor to him?" (1Cor. 11:14).

The Torah then prescribes a sufficiency of means for the vital service of the priesthood. Although the Levites were not to own a portion of the Land (for the Lord is their portion), they were to receive the first fruits of the sacrifice and the tithe, just as did the priests who served the other functions. While this may be unsettling for those who desire their worship teams to be made up of all volunteers—often while the pastor has his needs met, and sometimes to excess—let us stay with the biblical facts on principle: Nowhere does the Torah 'demote' the ministry of music to beneath that of the sacrificial and administrative functions (analogous to today's pastor).

Training

As we see that God chose to work the redemption of music out through a trained and holy group of professional musicians, priests, and prophets, we should look at what is involved in training in the parallel fields of today.

Perhaps the most demanding undergraduate degree is that in a music-related discipline. In addition to the normal academic core requirements, one is expected to gain a mastery of at least one and preferably more instruments, and to remain active in a number of unpaid performing groups. Studies done have equated the skill level needed to obtain a bachelor's degree in composition, for example, as meeting or exceeding those needed for a Ph.D. in engineering, another demanding field. Excellence in the musical discipline requires not just the casual hobbyists, but trained artisans, today, and in biblical times.

In the sacred realm a musician should also be studied in the scriptures. Either in choosing appropriate music or in composing it, far too often cutesy folk renderings with watered-down doctrine, cliché popular formulas, or both, pass for 'inspirational' music. Often, because of budgetary restrictions and other factors, the production value of such music also is well behind what is found in the secular realm. The result is music that sounds like a poor imitation of a popular genre. While this doesn't describe all modern sacred music, it is a noticeable trend and therefore should be cited. One would be hard pressed today to find a church where anything approaching art or classical music may be heard on a regular basis.

Further, consistent quality of execution requires continual outside study or practice. As one prominent concert artist remarked, "If I don't practice for one day, I notice it. If I don't practice for two days, my audience notices."[1] The primary reason that the better music today is outside the realm of Godliness is that the secular forces recognize and appreciate the power of this art form, and they reward their champions gloriously. The church often fails to recognize even the basic need for sustenance of her skilled performers and the results are tragic. Either the skilled players are driven out by less dedicated artisans, or they are forced to compromise their level of quality in working within tight budgetary constrictions. With these observations I don't desire to "lay down the law," (as that has already been done by a much greater authority), but to observe Bible facts and principles for growth, which is undoubtedly needed.

The better Christian artists of today are able to receive some sustenance through the free-market system. This,

---

[1] Proverbial, reference unavailable.

however, is not the preferred means of compensation, biblically or historically. Such a democratic system effectively puts the consumer in the role of a "creative censor." An artist who responds to market forces in order to put bread on the table is more likely to compromise his message for popular support than one with other means of sustenance. Consider if the writing of scripture had been left to public consensus. The free-market force was the economic key to the romantic revolution in the arts. With it came a shift from a music that served to exalt the Creator to one that came to worship 'art' and the 'artist.' Thus began the departure from the Baroque and Classical period ethos which, being supported by church, royal, and private patronages, served more to exalt God.

Given that the ideal is not likely to occur in the near future, a few observations are in order regarding the means by which artists do survive today. *Copyright* law is designed to protect the creative property of those producing original music recordings, books, etc. With the burgeoning technology of the last fifty years it has become increasingly easy to reproduce and enjoy these creative mediums without purchasing anything from which the creative artist will benefit. However, the responsible consumer of today should consider that his favorite artist is dependant upon these purchases for their sustenance and that such participation is minimal in the light of the benefits received. This is especially true today, when an artist who refuses to 'sell out' faces overwhelming odds to make it.

Ultimately, the artist stands in the role of 'priest and prophet' to his following, and both audience and artist are therefore worthy of their due consideration.

Qualities to Look for in an Artist

Personal
- Espouses and lives out values that you can embrace
- Avoids using overt or subtle messages of corruption
- Is wholehearted in his work
- Is submitted to God
- Is clean in manner and appearance

Musical
- Makes good use of melody
- Avoids overly repetitive use of rhythm
- Is a skilled writer and/or performer
- Is well studied in the subjects that he addresses
- Takes *innovative* risks

Levels of Musicianship

- Theorist/Philosopher
- Composer/Creator
- Performer

Musical Prophet: Combines All Three Levels.

6

The Music of the Prophets

There exists in our time, an urgent sense among many that some important part is missing, or lost, from the pages of the scriptures. Some have sought out new meaning through studying mystical Hebrew 'codes' and by pursuing sensationalized discoveries such as the Dead Sea Scrolls. Others have developed novel approaches to hermeneutics, or interpretive systems, in attempting to draw new insight from the Holy writ. Although intently pursued, none of the heralded discoveries or approaches have lived-up to their billing, nor satisfied the desire for a deeper revelation of God's will that exists within the religious community.

A previously untapped area, and one in which recent scholarship has provided an exciting breakthrough, is seen in the deciphering of the *musicality* of the Hebrew Bible by twentieth-century French musicologist Suzanne Haik-Vantoura. This discovery has the legitimate potential to provide for greater understandings of the Bible in both the short and the long-term.

It is known from history and the Bible that Moses, David, and Solomon wrote music, and that music was a part of the activities of the schools of the prophets (see 1Sam. 10:5). It has been historically thought that only the literature produced by these ancient men of faith had survived, their music being lamentably lost in history. We now know that this is not necessarily the case, that many of the Bible writer's most important melodies may have been preserved in the form of an ancient music notation existing within the very pages of the Hebrew 'Masoretic' text.

In looking at this discovery we will be addressing two main issues: the correct means by which to interpret the notation, with its theological implications; and its probable originators, according to the best available evidences, the prophets themselves. We will overview Haik-Vantoura's extensive work, and her revolutionary 'key' that unlocks this biblical music. The 'art music' tradition of ancient Israel, while setting the tone for national worship, was distinct from the simpler 'folk traditions' used in the surrounding synagogues.

Although Mme. Vantoura's comprehensive work has out-reached a vast majority of contemporary scholars, (though praised by some of the most eminent), the layman will be able to comprehend the simple beauty and logic of this recovered art through our overview. We will also offer exciting new insights and proofs relative to this discovery.

The Masoretes

We begin our study with the Hebrew Masoretic text, which is the accepted text used by scholars for Bible translation and interpretation.

Published just prior to the tenth century by the scribes of Tiberias (in northern Israel), the text contains all that is necessary to read, pronounce, and interpret the sacred writ. Included are 1) the consonantal Hebrew letters, 2) the vowel points and 3) the cantillation marks (or *te'amim*). The latter two elements of the text are thought to have been the 'oral tradition' accompanying the scriptures previous to their being recorded by the scribes. As we shall see, this view of an oral transmission is not likely to be accurate.

The term *Masorete* derives from the Hebrew word *Masorah*, which means 'tradition' and refers to the collected body of instructions used within Judaism to preserve the layout and text of the Bible. The effectiveness of these instructions is such that the biblical text has been preserved intact throughout history. Except for minor points of spelling, or details of vocalization and accentuation, and in comparison to transmissions of other Jewish literature, the Bible is virtually perfect.

In the Torah scrolls used in synagogues throughout the centuries, it is the consonantal letters that are recorded, absent are the vowels and cantillation marks. Prior to reading publicly from the scrolls, the *Chazzan* (Cantor) *prepares* by studying 'codices' that contain the accents and vowel markings, and interprets them according to his own particular tradition. These interpretations vary from sect to sect both in view of the vowel points and the *te'amim* (musical accents). It is, however, in the case of the *te'amim* that by far the greatest differences and questions exist in terms of interpretive approach. The differences in approach to the vowels are, by comparison, negligible within the differing Jewish sects.

The Hebrew letters of the Bible are printed in block form. This is the equivalent of our printed consonants. A study of what is contained here is enough to fill many volumes. For our purposes it will suffice to observe that the letters of the Hebrew alphabet are pictorial and self-descriptive in nature. For instance, the first letter, *Aleph* א, represents the Ox, and roughly looks as such with the horn-like protrusions of the letter. Similarly so for the letter *Bet* ב (house), *Gimel* ג (camel), and so forth.

Surrounding the consonants below, above, and within the letters are the vowels points. They also are pictorial and have names describing their respective functions. The purpose of the vowel markings is to maintain the complex system of Hebrew grammar, showing us how to correctly pronounce the words and phrases. The nineteen te`amim also are placed above and below the consonantal alphabet and are the equivalent of the punctuation of the text and, as we shall see, much more. They also are pictographic and have ancient names depicting their function. We will now focus our study on these latter markings.

The plural noun *te`amim* comes from the verb *ta`am*, "to taste or discern." A well known biblical reference makes use of this word. In Psalm 34:8, David enjoins us to *"taste* (ta`am) the Lord," to see that He is good.

As has been noted, no universally accepted approach exists regarding the interpretation of the te`amim since their publication. Indeed, no self-consistent approach has existed throughout this same time, where the meaning and usage of a particular symbol has been consistent throughout the text.

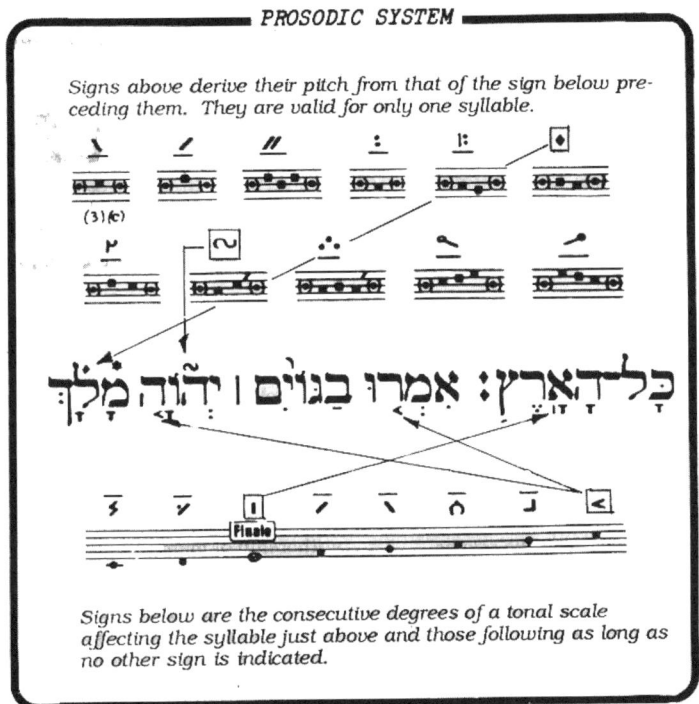

Fig. 1- Te`amim as they appear within Hebrew Bible
By Gene Fakler, Associates for Biblical Research, from article "Music of the Temple" by John Wheeler (ABR, Winter 1989, p14).

Further, none of the existing systems have accounted for the principles of name, shape, and function that apply to the other elements of the Hebrew language. It may therefore be concluded that, at least from the time of the Masoretes, the understanding of these symbols was lost. As pure logic would dictate, the very existence of nineteen different symbols would, as music, require more fluctuation of pitch than just the fourth or fifth intervals prominently used in the various 'formula' renderings of the synagogue traditions.

A Musical/ Poetic Approach

The question then arises as to why and how the interpretation being presented and favored here is different from those of the past 1100 years. Simply stated, the scholars who had previously attempted to interpret the notation were primarily grammarians and theologians. This is akin to handing a score of a Mozart concerto to a neurosurgeon, untrained in Western music, and then asking him for an interpretation! A creative view may result, but unlikely an accurate one. The failure to recognize the notation as being primarily musical was the main handicap for these scholars. However, musicians attempting to solve the notation overlooked the importance of the grammatical 'template,' the verbal syntax of the Hebrew text. As is characteristic of inspired thought, it was by assimilating the two approaches that Haik-Vantoura solved the age-old puzzle (the right starting premise being the musicality of the signs, *and* with the right template of the biblical verbal syntax).

"It was by this process that [Suzanne] was able to identify the functions of the sublinear and superlinear signs within each of two different yet related systems of te'amim (the prosodic and psalmodic systems) found in the Masoretic Text. The sublinear signs in each system represent the degrees of a diatonic or altered diatonic scale, the superlinear signs, embellishments to the melody defined by the sublinear signs."[1] What resulted after much scientific experimentation was a tight-fitting melodic language that corresponds to the verbal syntax and message of the Bible throughout the text, and one that is uniquely self-consistent.

---

[1] John Wheeler, *King David' s Harp Inc.*

Chironomy

Next came the crowning corroboration of the ancient symbols' names with their newly discovered functions, and their shapes to the ancient gestural method of conducting called chironomy.

An example of the logic behind the names of the scale degrees is found in the lower sign, *Silluq* meaning 'end' which equates to our tonic. The name requires little imagination and indeed it seems odd that none picked up on these clues previously. Haik-Vantoura also surmised that the lower sign (representing a scale tone) must continue until interrupted by an upper sign (ornament) and then must return to the last lower sign.

The system is supported by historical and biblical references. The pictorial nature of the symbols dates back to the ancient practice of chironomy, which is the use of hand signals to convey musical value. This can be seen in Egyptian art depicting one or more conductors signaling to musicians. Various such systems are in use today as in the western tradition of solfedge (Do Re Me . . .). Note also the similarity of our words for 'sign' and 'sing.' The same letters are used, only slightly rearranged, indicating the close conceptual relationship even within the modern English syntax.

The Bible itself is pointing to this practice (1Chron. 25:1-6) when it states that the psalms were conducted "upon the *hands* of Asaph" (Also see Ezra 3:10).

(A student of Haik-Vantoura, John Wheeler took the initiative to reconstruct the complete gestural conducting system for the *te'amim*. The restoration of this ancient music is therefore in theory, complete.)

What is not specified in the notation that we might see as lacking are the 'accidentals' indicating which mode or scale is to be utilized. You may know to play or sing the 3rd degree of the scale, for instance, but is it major or minor? This too is answered through ancient music traditions in which the musical mode would be adjusted in performance to fit the 'mood' of the text and would have been common knowledge amongst the performers. Along with deriving appropriate accompaniment, determining the appropriate mode involves the artistic sensibilities more so than other parts of the 'realization' process, which are more easily made objective.[1] (It is interesting also to note that as there are seven primary 'modes' in music, there are also seven verb 'moods' in biblical Hebrew.)

Ancient music in general is thought to have been primarily that of a melody supporting some form of prose. This is exactly what the Masoretes have transmitted. Any accompaniment would have been a simple one and added to the fixed melody based on the accepted norms of the time. The rhythm is derived from the text, and in the case of psalmody, a simple meter (regular tempo) is added.

Something that troubled the musicologists was Haik-Vantoura's assertion that the ancient Hebrews used the full seven-tone scale. This should not be so surprising as it was the ancient Pythagorus that is credited with discovering the physics of the overtone series that produces these intervals, and, given that the ancient cultures represented advanced civilizations, their full use of this musical system should be expected more so than not.

With these conclusions, we now, in studying the Hebrew Bible, are faced not only with an advanced linguistic syntax as had been commonly known amongst

---

[1] Musicians hoping to reconstruct these melodies are advised to obtain the realized scores as they become available through this ministry and to study Mme. Vantoura's comprehensive thesis for more insight.

the scholars, but also an advanced and subtle music to accompany it. This none dared to hope for!

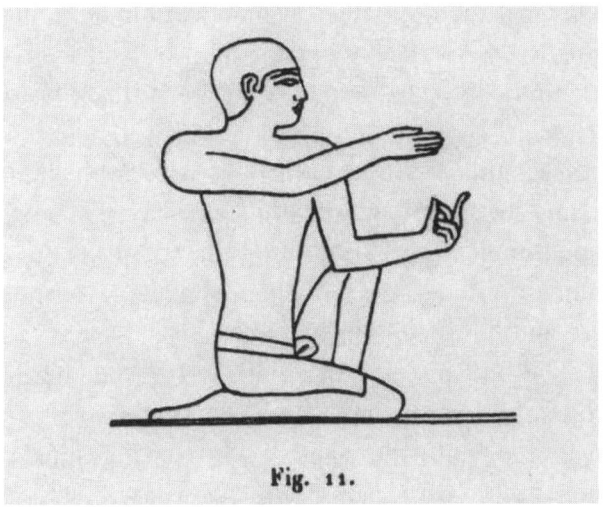

Fig. 2- Egyptian Chironomist- 'Sign and Sing'
Hickman, from cover of *Archaeology and Biblical Research,* Autumn, 1989.

Two Notational Systems

The timing of the publication of the Masoretic text is most telling as well. In the Middle Age we see a reflowering of music within the established Christian church. Modern western notation began to be created as a way to preserve this newly advancing art. This gradual development has been well documented. The ninth century theoretician Boethius began developing a crude system, followed by a monk named Hucbald in the tenth century, then a Benedictine monk named Guido who formalized the system of lines and spaces that we use today in western tradition. Thus it was through an evolutionary and logical *process* that modern musical notation was born.[1]

It is important to note that written notation responded to the need to communicate musical ideas accurately through time and with the awareness that human memory, unaided, was not up to the task. As is aptly stated in a Chinese proverb, "the strongest memory is weaker than the weakest ink."[2]

The fact that the Masoretic text was published at the same time that the western system had become fully developed indicates that the Jewish scribes were likely responding to the rival Christian Church and sought to preserve and advance their own, already developed, sacred liturgy. The fundamental difference to be noted here is that the Hebraic system appeared upon the scene fully developed, as "out of nowhere," not over a gradual period of time as the western system. We now know that it represents an advanced art-music as well.

The recovered music must challenge the conventional wisdom that the system of vowels and accents were maintained orally up until their sudden publication in the tenth century. Such an idea is at this point a statistical improbability. The complexity and accuracy of the te`amim alone would make the idea of an oral transmission of the music an absurdity. The complex system of grammar contained within the vowel points doubles this improbability, as it also is a fully developed and scholarly syntax.

Consider, for instance, the transmission of Shakespearian English, something that has been all but lost in practice

---

[1] James, Jamie. *Music of the Shperes*. New York: Copernicus Springer-Verlag, 1995, p. 80-81.
[2] Shoemaker, Samuel Moore, Jr. *The Conversion of the Church*. Fleming H. Revell, 1932.

over a period of just a few hundred years even *with* an existing written tradition to maintain its grammar. Yet we are told that the grammar of the Hebrew Bible was maintained more or less intact by oral tradition for 2500-3500 years! This is highly unlikely, to say the least.

As for the fully developed system of music, this too challenges the conventional wisdom regarding its conveyance. As any musicologist is aware, musical systems are not created at will and cannot be generated overnight. Even with the use of modern computers, such attempts generally produce more noise than subtle forms of art.

Going back to the chronology, we know that it took roughly 700 years from the development of western *written* tradition to produce a J.S. Bach, another 100 years to produce a Mozart, then Beethoven, then Chopin, etc. Each musical giant necessarily built upon the work of all those who went before, and none could have existed in history on their own,[1] and certainly not without a written tradition by which to convey their ideas. How could it possibly be that the Hebrew culture could have orally transmitted and/or invented such fully developed systems of music and grammar without the aid of both a written tradition and a prolonged period of time in which to accomplish such formidable feats (i.e., the time span needed for the writing of the Old Testament revelation)? We must then agree with Haik-Vantoura, that somehow these systems came to the Masoretes in written form and were merely transcribed and published by them.

---

[1] Johann Sebastian Bach arguably produced the most unique and original art music. Although summarizing the best of Baroque style, his music is in a class of its own. A consistently high quality of music with a complexity of harmonic material that rivals that of the most modern composers, Bach's music is a phenomenon to be contemplated and enjoyed by those of all subsequent eras.

Music, Spirit, and the Keys to Prophecy

Upper Signs (all rows left to right)
Ornaments, found above the text.

Lower Signs (main pitch), found below text (1st vertical row as numbered)

Te`amim application chart- Prosody
Used for all books excepting the Psalmodic books.
Music of the Bible Revealed –Suzanne Haik-Vantoura

The Lost Music of the Prophets

Upper Signs (all rows left to right)

Lower Signs (1st row verticle as numbered)

Te`amim Application Chart- Psalmody
Used for the Psalms, Proverbs, and the body of Job.
Music of the Bible Revealed-Suzanne Haik-Vantoura

Prophetic Styles

A strong piece of evidence for the authorship of the biblical melodies involves the musical styles of the various melodies. Just as a good original composer or author of today has a style that he may be identified by, so it is with the biblical writers. At a time when liberal scholarship is challenging the authorship of various books of the Bible,[1] Haik-Vantoura's restoration reveals subtle musical styles that actually support the traditional views of authorship. Through her many realizations of the melodies, including all 150 Psalms, Mme. Vantoura observed unique melodic styles consistent with the various attributions found in the Psalm titles: to David, Asaph, Moses, Solomon, Heman, and the Sons of Korah, respectively.

Having gained experience with the Mosaic texts as well as the prophet Isaiah and the Psalms, this author heartily concurs with these findings. Noticeable styles of expression do distinguish the different books.

In light of the fact that ancient prose generally was considered to be delivered with a melody, an interesting question arises. Would God's revelation to His prophets, being so meticulously constructed from every other angle, have been left to an uninspired rendering in the musical sense, the main 'vehicle' for its presentation? Common sense alone would dictate that He would have correspondingly given inspired melodies. Any other

---

[1] A prime example of this phenomenon is seen in the book called *The Book of J*. This product of modern liberal 'scholarship' seems intended to bring doubt and confusion to the study of God's word amongst the naïve and biblically illiterate. Its main thesis is to assert that the 'attributes' of God that are described by Moses, using His various names (Elohim, YHVH), are actually evidences of separate writers perhaps describing God in their own way. Not only does this theory of multiple authors militate against the preponderance of historic sources, but also linguistic evidence, and now perhaps most convincingly, the musical/melodic proofs.

rendering, it may be argued, could be seen as 'adding to' the revelation of scripture by the prophets and therefore unthinkable. With the evidence herein represented—even that of the perfectly fitting melodies themselves—some pressure must be asserted on the scholars of today to begin to answer to such compelling assertions.

It should also be noted that this study represents a 'non-mystical' approach to Bible interpretation. There is no manipulation of characters such as letter skips, contortions or other distortions of the sacred text as required in approaches such as 'Bible-code' theologies. The only thing required is to correctly read and interpret an ancient melodic notation, as it appears in the text, and in 'synchronicity' with the language of the Bible itself.

The 'Holy Grail'

When taken in total, the music that we are discussing may rightly be called the 'Holy Grail' of Old Testament interpretation. By the embellishing of key words and phrases with musical ornaments,[1] to providing a 'perfect punctuation' to the text (without which there is *no* punctuation), to the answering of questions anomalies within the text, the music indeed gives the scripture its fullest expression.

The exegetical implications of this music are most interesting. Observe within the English language how the punctuation serves to define and interpret the meaning of the text. The ability for a comma to turn around a meaning in the English such as "Don't stop" or "Don't, stop" suggests a great potential for the value of this 'musical punctuation' of the Bible. As an example, Isaiah 16:4 may be rendered "Let the outcasts of Moab…" or, as the

---

[1] See Appendix 1 for a demonstration of this phenomenon.

te'amim would indicate, "Let My outcasts, O Moab." How much clearer is the message then, when delivered with a melody that matches the emotional and spiritual intent of the author? (Also to be observed by anyone who works with this musical system is an intricacy of construction so precise that it is capable of falling apart if one element within a phrase is misinterpreted.)

Another ancient eastern language one may reference is that of Chinese. Here, the tonal inflection used with a word or phrase literally determines its meaning. The same word may thereby convey completely diverse meanings. The tonal nature of biblical Hebrew is a like scenario, though far more sophisticated and precise in its use of tonal variety.

Within the music of the Bible, we see the subtle use of musical devices such as repetition and melodic imagery. When there is a repeated verbal idea, such as the enumeration of the days of the week in the Genesis Creation account ("the evening and the morning . . ."), there is also a repeated melody that unifies the theme. This device is strikingly used in Psalm 136 and the phrase *ki le olam chasdo*, or "because His mercy endures forever." The statement concludes each of the 26 verses of the Psalm and is consistently sung with the same melody (outlining a root-position triad). This might be seen as an unnecessary redundancy until we stop and look at the important concept being asserted. The musical device adds great emphasis to the Psalmist's important point regarding his ever-merciful God.

(Apart from being merely repetitive, the number 26 is representative of the heavenly order, where the 24 elders worship before the Father and Son (Rev. 5:8). Not 27 as if the Holy Spirit were a 'person' worthy of worship. It is also the numeric value of the personal name of God (YHVH) according to the Hebrew gematria).

Appealing to the melody of the text also solves grammatical problems that have puzzled scholars throughout the centuries. Certain Torah passages appear to use wrong gender pronouns, not agreeing with their objects. Haik-Vantoura has observed that the melodic ornaments to these passages are the reason for these anomalies, not poor grammar on the part of the scribes. The difference of one syllable between the Hebrew *lakh* (fem.) and *lekha* (masc.) can make all the difference to a songwriter, as may be witnessed in the many modern pieces that change normal grammar usage to accommodate a particular melodic line. It was none the less so for the biblical writers.

The music may ultimately explain why there was no need to *debate* the meaning of the Bible when it was read to ancient Israel. The people, when the Bible was read (sung) to them, immediately proclaimed their "obedience" (the only thing then in question as the *meaning* was clear), and they "wept" (Exod. 24:7, Neh. 8:8). What could better explain such a phenomenon than the reading being one that was *sung* in the original language using the proper inflection and accentuation?

Biblical Proofs

Internally, the Bible itself speaks of this music. The psalmist David wrote, "thy *statutes* are my songs" (Ps. 119:54). It is in the Torah that the statutes of God are contained, not the Psalms, and they are something that David was apparently singing. The Hebrew word used here for song is *zemirot*,[1] which further indicates that they were

---

[1] Strong's #2158. *The New Strong's Exhaustive Concordance of the Bible*. Thomas Nelson Publishers. Kansas City. 1990

accompanied melodies, in contrast to traditional chants that are rendered unaccompanied in synagogue practice.

(In my experience with the biblical melodies I have found that they can work quite well with accompaniment, even in a contemporary style. Here I come into conflict with both traditionalism and some ancient music purists. I yet maintain, and believe my arrangements prove out, that this music [like all great music] is timeless, and adaptable to diverse settings of style.)

The scriptures also clearly define the *writing* of God's inspiration generally: "Thus speaketh the Lord God of Israel, saying, *Write* thee all the words that I have spoken unto thee in a book." (Jer. 30:2). "And the Lord answered me, and said, *Write* the vision, and make it plain upon tables, that he may run that readeth it." (Hab. 2:2). The Bible mentions a written form of music at the time of Moses, "Now therefore, *write* down this song"(Deut. 31:19). This command obviously could not have been given without the existence of a written notation, or the ever-precise Bible would have read, "write down this *lyric, * and make up your own melody."

In the Song of the Red Sea (Exod. 15), we see the earliest form of biblical melody recorded in the Bible, a simple form of music that then developed in complexity as the scriptural revelation proceeded. Also, when biblical writers quoted Moses, the te'amim indicate that they did so using his melody and their own melodic ornaments (as in Isa. 12:2, 12:4).

Historical writings and commentaries within Jewish tradition are indicative of this music as well. The Babylonian Talmud states that the Bible should be read "only with its melody" (Megilla 32a). This is a strong statement for their importance from the Jewish sources.

The commentary from the Talmud on Eccl. 12:9 interprets the phrase "with knowledge" as meaning that Solomon taught the people the law with its accents. The *Mahzor Vitry* compiled in 1100C.E. states that the meaning of the musical signs "was revealed to Moses on Sinai."[1] This indicates a very authoritative source for the markings indeed!

Words alone fall short of describing the musical experience, let alone the spiritual. Many in history have refused to write about music on this basis, claiming that the art 'speaks' well enough for itself. Attempting to describe spiritual realities with mere words can be similarly difficult.

Given such a correlation, wouldn't the Creator of the universe naturally inspire music along with His word in order to better convey the spiritual realities to an earthbound people? Indeed, as the very words of the Bible speak of its being inspired, so too does the existence of this music speak for its having been divinely influenced.

The next question we must ask is how and from where did this written notation come? If the Masoretes transmitted the tradition without understanding its true meaning, where and how did they receive it? As advanced and perfectly preserved as it is, the odds do not favor an oral tradition, but a more fixed, written tradition being handed down over time. But where is the evidence? No complete manuscripts exist pre-dating the Masoretes.

The Prophetic Lineage Confirmed

The most decisive clue as to how this notation could have been transmitted is found in a much-overlooked poem

---

[1] *Mahzor Vitry*, copied by Rabbi Simha de Vitry, from *The Music of the Bible Revealed*, p.65

by the Masorete writer Moses ben Asher. As observed by John Wheeler, the "Song of the Vine" identifies the "Elders of Bathyra" of 200B.C.E. as being "the heirs to the prophets" possessing "knowledge of understanding" who *established* the accents of scripture.[1] This family of priests reigned in Israel after the Babylonian captivity and at a time when the Greek conqueror Antiochus Epiphanes was trying to destroy the prophetic worship of Israel. According to ben Asher, the Elders of Bathyra preserved the poetry and music of the Bible by then writing it down, once again.[2] We know from history that the Sanhedrin removed the Elders of Bathyra from service just prior to the time of Christ. Here are excerpts from this all-telling Masoretic poem:[3]

Line 1: "Thou {God} hast planted a precious stock of vine…"

Line 4: "The branches of the vine are the Prophets…"

Line 22: "The perfect ones of the vine are the Elders of Bathyra, the heirs of the prophets, who posses knowledge of understanding."

Line 24: "As delights they have established the accents of Scripture (hitqinu *ta`ame* miqra), giving sense and interpreting its word."

Line 25: "They have erected as a fence round the Torah of our God, well-arranged Masoras [or traditions] to instruct the ignorant."

Line 28: "Afflictions surrounded them from the kings of the Greeks and exiled them and dispersed them to No (Egypt) and its provinces."

---

[1] Haik-Vantoura. *The Music of the Bible Revealed*, Berkely. Bibal Press and King David's Harp Inc. 1991, p501 postface.

[2] Note that the destruction of both Jewish Temples were, in part, attacks on the Israelite music ministry, this is a poignant comment on the essence of this battle.

[3] Ibid. p 501.(Translation by Paul Kahle).

A poignant observation made by Haik-Vantoura is that the edict to "build a fence around the Torah" from this era probably originated with the priestly family the *Elders of Bathyra* and not with the Jewish military leader *Matthias Macabees* as has been traditionally thought. In this light, one might observe that the shapes of the te`amim make them appear as variously angled fence-posts that literally *surround* the letters of the Torah (see fig.1). Jewish tradition, much of which is rabbinic and not biblical in origin has been considered the object of that edict throughout much of history. In light of the preceding evidence, I would concur with Haik-Vantoura, that *the musical/ poetic liturgy* is the most direct object of that reference, and not Jewish tradition in general.

Returning to the subject of the transmission of the notation, it is noteworthy that the Levitical priests maintained the prophetic traditions from the Macabeen time until they began to be dispersed after the Romans destroyed the second temple in 70A.D.

History leaves no other clues of this notation until the eighth century when scrolls found outside a cave in Jericho were brought to the ruling *Karaite* Jews in Jerusalem. Within fifty years of that discovery, the complete Hebrew text of words and accents that we have today appears as "out of nowhere."[1] These scrolls may well have contained the lost or hidden traditions that the Masoretes then published.

The importance of the *Karaite* involvement in the publishing of the *Masorah* should not be overlooked. Their name comes from the Hebrew *b'nai mikra*, which means "sons of the reading" (of the book). They held that only the scriptures were valid for Jewish doctrine and were opposed

---

[1] John Wheeler, *King David' s Harp Inc.* Houston, TX.

to rabbinic authority, which they were only able to displace for a time in the eighth century. The Masorete scribes were also *Karaites*. This would place each in the lineage of the prophets in terms of the transmission of their traditions. These traditions have been miraculously preserved through history and now may once again be marveled at and enjoyed.

Here, then is an outline of this 'lineage of the Prophets' and the keepers of their sacred traditions:

- Biblical Prophets: Moses to Malachi
- King David, Levites
- Solomon and the First Temple
- The Return from Babylon. The Elders of Bathyra who "established the accents of Scripture," the fence around the Torah, during attack of Antiochus Epiphanes 156 B.C.
- Levites and the Second Jerusalem Temple
- 70 A.D. Temple sacked and understanding of music becoming lost.
- 850 A.D. Scrolls found in cave in Jericho, brought to Jerusalem Karaites.
- 900 A.D. Masoretic text published with complete vowels and accents as "out of nowhere"

The Lost Music of the Prophets

- 1975 *Musique de la Bible Revelee*, S.H. Vantoura recovers musical meaning of the te`amim.
- Future Use? (see chapter 9, the Two Witnesses).

The history of this music is of its being given, being used in public ministry, then being secreted away and preserved during persecution and conquest, then of re-emergence. Its preservation is proof of God's faithfulness to maintain all the elements of His revelation to man through time, and the faithfulness of a few chosen messengers to cooperate with that plan.

A Hidden Message

Despite her extensive work, Mme. Haik-Vantoura failed to observe many of the New Testament theological and prophetic implications of her discovery. Not the least among these is an important message stated by the music itself. As seen in the preceding te-amim charts, the tonic note for the Hebrew modes occurs at the third scale degree. This means that in application, *the scale resolves to the tonic from below.*

6 7 <u>1</u> 2 3 4 5 6
Scale Structure of Te`amim
Resolves to the tonic from seventh below.

As we know from our chapter on the musical scale meta-type, resolving to the *octave* (the tonic above) symbolizes spiritual elevation and renewal. Haik-Vantoura's discovery here proves itself to be theologically correct in a surprising way. Despite the inspired imagery and artistry of the Hebraic music, we may know by the very structure of the modes themselves that one may not be sufficiently *renewed* through Moses and the prophets alone. These melodies only go to the *octave* as a foretaste and anticipation, but to resolve, must go back to the tonic from the seventh below. In order to finally ascend to the *octave*, one must look to a future covenant, the New Testament and the atonement offered to all by Jesus the Messiah, the New Song, and the ultimate resolution, whose name value is 888. It is here, and here alone that we find renewal and the ultimate resolution to the human drama, theologically, musically, and spiritually. The New Testament revelation therefore contains the resolution that all the biblical Hebrew music played to and anticipated.

<u>1</u> 2 3 4 5 6 7 <u>8</u>
Scale from natural overtone series
Ascension and resolution to octave.

Notice in this context the following statement pertaining to the Old Testament saints who understood and anticipated this same resolution.

"These all died in faith, not having received the promises, but having *seen them afar off* were assured of them, embraced them, and confessed that they were stranger and pilgrims on the earth." Heb. 11:13 (it. added)

7

Traditions of Men, of God

The question of what constitutes the true traditions of the biblical faith is at the heart of the religious struggle as seen throughout the centuries and therefore requires a closer look.

The word 'tradition', found only in the New Testament comes from the Greek *paradosis*, meaning to "entrust or transmit." The New Testament usage has both positive and negative connotations. Christ taught that the traditions of *men* make the word of God void and are to be shunned by the believer (Matt. 15:6). He repeatedly rebuked the religious community of Israel on this point. The apostle Paul, however, wrote to the Thessalonians to 'hold to' the traditions that they had been taught "by word or letter" (2 Th. 2:15).

The obvious indication is to discern those that pertain to the word of God and those that somehow subvert its authority. This issue has never been more pertinent than in our day. Many believers today are discovering the fact that pagan traditions have found their way into the Christian church e.g., Easter (from *Ishtar*, the fertility goddess) and Christmas (the winter solstice) celebrations. Historically, these anomalies trace back to compromises made with paganism after Emperor Constantine and the formation of the Roman 'State' church. As believers gain more historical insight, a sort of reformation is taking place with a return to biblical Hebraic identity.

Metaphors and Rabbinism

Traditional Jewish practices are thus being adopted by many Christians today. Here the terrain gets steep as to what is and is not biblical. The Jewish sect of *Karaism*, which rejects rabbinic authority and follows what they believe is a more biblically observant lifestyle have abandoned many traditions that Messianic Christians have adopted. Some of the *Karaite* wisdom should be examined in this regard.

Fallacies in the traditional uses of *mezuzot* (doorpost ornaments), and *tefillin* (prayer boxes), are exposed. The scriptures that supposedly command such practice in truth have a more metaphoric significance. For instance, having an ornament on the doorpost of your house (" . . . you shall write them on the . . .") does not get at the heart of the commandment to "love the Lord" and to keep His commandments (Deut. 6). Placing a person on one's chest, "Set me as a seal upon your heart" (Song of Sol. 8:6) would be a difficult project, if one favors the literal rendering for such scriptures.

It has been the lesson of history that what people wanted to take from scripture as metaphoric was often more literal, such as the virgin birth of the Messiah, and what they understood to be literal was often metaphoric. Remember, God is the ultimate dramatist and He uses all such elements to convey His message. In this light, the possibility should be considered that the traditions the ancient *Karaites* transmitted, those of the vowel points, te'amim, and the rules for transmitting the scriptures generally, are the very traditions that holy men have referenced throughout history and not those of a more rabbinic variety.

Compare Paul's comments on the fruit of the Spirit with the external practices. "But the fruit of the Spirit is love, joy, peace, longsuffering, kindness, goodness, faithfulness, gentleness, self-control" (Gal. 5:22). The obvious contrast here is the focus being on inward observance as opposed to mere outward appearance. In contrast, the music and poetry of the Bible does go to the heart when fully apprehended. (It is no accident that the word 'art' derives from 'heart'). I realize that I risk stepping on a lot of toes, but would encourage the reader to carefully consider this thesis before taking up an offense. Those who profit from selling mere religious decorations or who believe that by owning and displaying such they are truly serving God in righteousness ought to prayerfully reflect on the *spiritual* meaning of the scriptures they suppose they are thus fulfilling. True religion is first an internal matter, one of the heart, and not merely a cultural fashion statement.

The Hebrew Bible appears within the Christian tradition only after the sixteenth century and the Protestant reformation. Prior to that time the Greek Septuagint was considered to be authoritative based on the fact that the New Testament had been given in Greek. This view did not hold up over the course of time, due to anomalies discovered in the Greek translation (not the least of which was a flawed biblical chronology in which the Millennial Reign of Christ should have begun by around 500 A.D.).

The Torah and Its Hidden Traditions

We now take a look at a related tradition, passed down through history, which reinforces another misconception regarding the Hebrew Bible. It is traditionally considered that the Torah, which contain only the consonantal letters of the Hebrew, constitute the true and pure Bible, while the vowel points and *te'amim* (music), occupy a somewhat lesser status, that of a preserved *oral* tradition. I would like to suggest that this is not at all the case. In reviewing the prophetic lineage up to the Masoretes, it is evident that this publishing the consonants separately was done to preserve the *sanctity* of the "verbal and musical" syntax of the scriptures, not to demote them. Historical understanding, therefore, is completely backwards to the evidence at this point. The reason for this practice being carried out in the Jewish Diaspora was to prevent the Gentiles from profaning the sacred art traditions of the biblical text. The Torah scrolls therefore actually represent a kind of literary shorthand of the Bible, not necessarily the only 'pure' Bible.

'It's about the vowels'

In comparing elements of the Hebrew and Arabic languages, one may see the practical effectiveness of this approach. These ancient languages, developing geographically alongside each other are often identical in their use of consonants; however, vowel differences largely distinguish the two tongues.[1] (It is even said in Israel that if you learn one language, you know the next.)

Observe:

	Hebrew	*Arabic*
King	*melech*	*meliyk*
Father	*av (abba)*	*abu*
No	*loh*	*lah*
Peace	*shalom*	*salaam*

In the modern state of Israel, the Hebrew consonants alone are printed in publications such as newspapers, and it is then within the Jewish cultural context that one learns to "fill in" the necessary vowel inflections. The significant difference from the biblical tradition is that modern Israeli Hebrew is primarily *Ivrit kal*, or simple Hebrew whereas the language of the Bible is a fully developed scholarly and poetic syntax.

Scholars have shown similarities to Hebrew root words in many languages, not the least of which is English. Characteristically, it is the consonants that identify the words, and the vowels that are typically altered.

---

[1] Additionally, consider the name of the southern Jordanian town of *Acaba* (Arabic). By merely replacing the vowels, this may be rendered *Yacov* (Jacob), indicating the ancient Israelite presence in the area.

The vowels and accents, although a necessary part of the canon, were thus secreted away and are not traditionally included in the Torah scrolls proper. They are, even since their publication, put aside with secondary collections such as the *Chumashim* (reading portions) and other codexes, which also contain rabbinic commentary and more exclusively 'Jewish' doctrine. It is thus that the Holy language has been maintained within the Jewish cultural, and today predominantly rabbinic, context.

This should serve as a strong caution to the many Christians who are trying to gain a Hebraic understanding of the Bible by studying in such a context. Of course, care should be taken to avoid incorporating the non-biblical rabbinic teachings and concepts into the church.

Although this traditional means of preserving the sanctity of the language of the Bible has been maintained to this day, the understanding of why this is done has apparently been lost, or is still being obscured. Most Christian and Jewish Bible scholars still support the myth that the consonantal Hebrew text is the true Bible while the accents are a mere oral tradition that was fixed in form by the tenth century Masoretes.

The work of the Masoretes is, however, far more important than the mere documenting of one oral tradition of vocalizing the Bible. In fact the Masoretes appear to have transmitted the 'ultimate' way to express the Bible and one that must have also been given by the prophets in script. This is a weighty proposition whose evidence now needs to be fully considered by the scholars of today.

The necessary practice of secreting away the accents of Scripture, and continuance of the practice to date, easily explains the lack of manuscript evidence that would normally be expected to support a written tradition.

It is precisely because of the compromise of modern scholars on the point of the origin of these markings that the door has been opened to the many spurious notions surrounding the Hebrew Bible today. If the preserved grammar and music of the Bible only represent a mere oral tradition, then one gives up the authority to confront the errors of those seeking out mystical codes or devising alternate new pronunciations for the sacred texts.

Alfred Eidersheim, writing at the end of the nineteenth century identifies a first century Temple music liturgy for the scriptural canon, although he mistakenly proclaimed the melodies to have been lost after the Temple destruction. In truth, the Masoretes had preserved them intact, and with the scholarship of Mme. Vantoura they may be fully understood once again. Hopefully through the efforts represented in this book, and in His strength, the awareness of these facts will build to more appropriate proportions, attracting the attention that such scholarship rightly demands.

Responses

Within the spiritual walk, one observes that an individual's measure of maturity is reflected in how he responds when confronted with new truth. With the unspiritual person and also the immature believer, there is seen a tendency toward anger, blame, self-righteousness, and even various strategies aimed at manipulation (Acts 8:18-20). The responses are then the survival tactics of the self, as one inevitably interprets the unknown as a threat to individuality

A healthy or mature response to truth involves first investigation, then humility and repentance (as there was likely a generous helping of the false residing in one previously), accompanied at some point by gratitude, support, and a desire to share the new revelation with others. If you don't use it, you lose it, as the saying goes.

A common statement that always takes on a very spiritual sounding tone is that of *"God is good to reveal this (new thing)."* The fact is that preserved or revealed truth throughout history normally comes at great sacrifice, and it is with much discipline that Godly people have persevered—not always because of, but often in spite of, the communities that they were serving. Revealing new truth, it may be said, takes a pioneering spirit. It was none the less so with the biblical prophets and the keepers of their traditions. In this context, consider Moses ben Asher's *Colophon of the Prophets*, translated by Paul Kahle.

I, Moses ben Asher have written this Codex of the Scripture according to my judgment "as the good hand of God was upon me" (Neh. II,8), "very clearly" (Deut XXVII,8), in the city of Ma'azya-Tabriya, "the renowned city" (Ezek. XXVI, 17), as it was understood by the congregation of Prophets, the chosen of the Lord, the saints of our God, who understood all hidden things and revealed the secret of wisdom, the oak trees of righteousness (Isa. LXI,3), the men of faith, who have concealed nothing of what was given to them nor added one word to what was transmitted to them, who have made the Scriptures powerful and mighty, the Twenty-four Books which they have founded in their faithfulness with explanatory accents and clear instruction as to pronunciation with sweet palate and beauty of speech. May it please our Creator to illuminate our eyes and enlighten our hearts by His Torah, that we may learn and teach and act with a perfect heart and a willing mind (I Chron. XXVIII,9) and for the whole of Israel, Amen![1]

---

[1] Haik-Vantoura. *The Music of the Bible Revealed*, Berkely. Bibal Press and King David's Harp Inc. 1991, p107.

8

The Sacred Name of God

The mysterious Tetragrammaton, or 'four-letter name' of God, has been the subject of much interest and debate throughout recorded history. Considered the 'ineffable,' or unpronounceable name of God, Jews throughout the centuries have shunned attempting to utter this word, while mystics and occultists have ascribed to it, hidden powers. Beneath the intrigue and debate, however, lies the story of a struggle to maintain the integrity of the Holy Scriptures and thus the intimate knowledge of the God of which they speak.

Having already established a basic understanding biblical Hebrew, we will begin with the grammatical features of the ancient Name of God, and offer a compelling resolution to the age-old mystery of its meaning and usage.

As the vowels and accents of the Hebrew Scriptures generally were secreted away (see chapter six) to keep them from being profaned by the Gentiles while Israel was in exile, those vowels specific to pronouncing the sacred, personal name of God were hidden in particular, even to the point of becoming completely lost.

Jewish tradition holds that יהוה (YHVH) should be rendered *Adonay* (Lord), or in some cases, *Elohim* (God) as in Ezekiel 47:13, when spoken. The vowels in the text, added as *substitutes* by the Masoretes, point to one or the other of these vocalizations. It is, in fact, impossible to read this word as written in the Hebrew, i.e., without using the Masorete's coding. The second letter "hey" (H) contains two contradictory vowel markings, the "o" above it and the "a" (or in some cases the "i") marking below it (as found in the authoritative Letteris edition). This was done in order to keep one from "profaning" the holy name of God by mispronouncing it and thereby transgressing His commandments. Jewish religious writers carry this tradition to the extreme by omitting the vowels when referencing the Deity even in English (i.e., *G-d* and *L-rd*).

Gentile translators, not being aware of this tradition, rendered the word with the vowels (however loosely) as *JeHoVaH*. Christians today, aware that something was lost in this translation, have become interested in reconstructing the correct Hebraic pronunciation of the Name. While this is a noble enough venture, what we have seen to this point has been a kind of counter dogmatism being advanced as a resolution this complex issue.

Examples of flawed scholarship abound in many of the popular books on the subject to date. These have in common authors who are self-taught and/or in an elementary level of Hebrew study. Many appear to have little experience with the principles of scriptural interpretation as well. We shall focus briefly on the kinds of errors being advanced in order to highlight some of the pitfalls of such scholarship. Not the least of which is the subtle undermining of the word of God through the false and misleading 'revelations' of the authors and supporters of these works.

In largely emotional appeals, some have promoted the idea that God's 'remnant' will consist of those who speak uniquely the Hebrew names of God. Such assertions when reasoned out are, of course, nonsensical. If indeed such practices were to define the remnant, then the church must include the Rastafarians, Masons, Cabbalists, and Occultists throughout history for their preoccupations with the Hebraic names of God. The Masonic manual *Morals and Dogma*, which no one could consider kosher for Christians, contains numerable references to God's Hebraic names. If anything will define the true remnant in the last days it will be that of holding to reasoned truth and sound doctrine, not the mere use of a supposed 'password' to the Almighty.

Some go so far as to say that the New Testament must be *flawed* (an implied claim of apostolic authority, and a dangerous theological line to cross) because it omits the Hebrew names. This is made over and against mountains of manuscript evidence that support the integrity of the Greek text, perhaps surpassing that of any other literature in history. For claims of New Testament flaws we should expect hard evidence, yet to date none has been produced, and certainly not the supposed 'lost original.'

The notion that one has a revelation from God, with the proof being "look at how strongly I feel about it" is more akin to Mormon doctrine, where truth is tested by a "burning in the bosom," than the historical Christian faith, which is supported by reasoned discourse and more sound biblical scholarship.

People are also being led to believe that they will experience a greater intimacy with God simply by pronouncing His name in the various authors' suggested fashions (*Yahweh* and *Yahuweh*, are popular versions). Even if it could be established that these various renderings of God's name were correct (and it cannot), such intimacy would, of course, be better gained from first having "clean hands and a pure heart" (Psalm 24:4).

Those asserting that the name Jesus is a derivative of Zeus, the Greek god, then transform the debate. Here again, however, the situation is in reverse. As we have established in our discussion on Hellenism (chapter one), it was the Greek philosophers who 'borrowed' their theologies from Moses, not vice versa. The theories that the apostles, or unscrupulous translators, corrupted the majority text of the New Testament ultimately seem aimed at casting doubt upon God's ability to preserve His Word through time—heresies to be sure.

The Masoretic pronunciation for Jesus' Hebrew name is *Yeshua*, from which *Iesous* in the Septuagint and Greek New Testament is derived. The name 'Jesus' then is a transliteration to English from the Greek.

Recall also, that it was God who created languages at the tower of Babel (Gen. 11:7). One who calls upon Him in any language will be heard, as surely a father knows the call of his children.

Apart from the view that one should not attempt to pronounce the Name, and the contrary opinion that you merit something by using a given pronunciation is, I believe, a more balanced approach.

Uses of 'Name'

The biblical uses of 'name' include that of appellation (a personal name), authority (in the name of), and presence (or person of). When we are told to revere and call upon the name of יהוה (the LORD) in scripture, the implication is thus variously of his *person*, *presence*, and *authority*. Given that the personal name of God has been obscured and even lost to most throughout history, it is only with a perverted view of His character that one would think its mere invocation overly important doctrine. The truths that are fundamental to the faith are yet apparent to the simplest of seekers and are sometimes lost on those that consider themselves to be wise (Luke 10:21).

Further, we see that God's names may be categorized according to type. The first in order of the least personal is the name *Adonay*. This is akin to the English 'Sir', and in Modern Hebrew it is roughly the equivalent. This is always appropriate when addressing a superior or to confer respect upon one deserving of such.

Next is *Elohim*, a kind of family name. This is the name *El* (God) in the plural sense (though simultaneously implying unity). The masculine plural form in Hebrew is chosen when any one of a grouping is male. This is the name used to describe God in His plurality such as in the Genesis Creation account. It is also used to describe His extended *family* of both the Old and New Testament, i.e.,

Israel and the Church: "I said 'You are gods (*Elohim*) and all of you are *children* of the Most High'" (Ps.82:6, John 10:34).

Then there is God's *personal name*, which He gave to Israel, יהוה (YHVH), and by extension ישוע *Yeshua* meaning "YHVH is salvation" (Matt. 1:21). The poetic diminutive form יה *Yah* is also used in scripture (as in Ps. 68:4). יהוה therefore is akin to a *first* name, and was given at a time in history when Israel was afforded such intimacy with their God. As the spiritual estrangement of national Israel grew, this name apparently fell into disuse, to the point of ultimately being lost, but only in terms of any authoritative vocalization. The nation that interacted with the Almighty on a first name basis in biblical times may, in general, only refer to Him as 'Sir' today. This is a sad but fitting description of the current spiritual state of God's chosen nation.

A New Look at the Name

It is important to make observations as to the obvious grammatical features of the Name. Recall that biblical Hebrew is a poetic language with an *advanced grammatical structure*. It is parallel to Shakespearean English in that regard. Any attempt therefore to recover the true pronunciation of the Name must respect this truth, observing all the known grammatical rules of the language.

The physical structure of biblical Hebrew consists of three main elements: consonants, vowels, and accent or punctuation marks. These equate to modern English in the following way:

Dnt stp	(consonants)
Dont stop	(w/vowels)
Don't, stop!	(w/vowels and punctuation)

The order of inspiration, rigor of transcription, and degrees of variance between manuscripts of the Hebrew text are: consonants, accents (*te`amim*), and vowel points.[1] The consonantal text of the Torah has been the most meticulously transmitted throughout history. In the Beatitudes (Matt. 5:17-18) Christ references this phenomenon in His stating "not one *jot* or *tittle* [or strokes that distinguish Hebrew letters] will pass from the law." Whereas there are but minor variances between existing Torah documents, we must conclude that He was referring to differences that would affect important doctrine. A slight hyperbole, if you will. Or, He was pointing to one of the several texts as being fully 'inerrant.'

This brings to mind the modern and misleading attempt to interpret the Bible by studying mystical Torah 'codes.' Rather than reading the text normally, these supposed 'scholars' attempt their readings of the Bible upside down, sideways, backwards, in intervals, etc., in order to find new meaning in the text. The results, at best, only are able to 'reveal' previously known, or assumed, facts.

The science behind this theory also is variously flawed. Any difference in the ordering of the consonants within the manuscripts completely changes the resultant code. As such variances are a given part of the scenery, and as the vowel markings are *omitted* in running the codes only later *adding the ones that are supportive* of one's preconceived thesis, this ball game is too loose to be considered by any serious scholar. If the vowels, likely being a part of the scripture,

---

[1] John Wheeler, King David's Harp Inc.

are included, the results would be far more limiting to the code theologians, even to the point of disproving their theses altogether.

Such focus also detracts from the more pertinent study of the poetry and music of the Hebrew Scriptures. Certainly, more clarity and insight is not to be gained by reading the Bible in contorted ways, but by better understanding the complexities of the poetic language and the musicality of the text. Ultimately too, the historic biblical faith is to be proven through living out its doctrines in daily life, not through the study of supposed 'codes.' This kind of practicality is apparently too mundane a task for many professing believers today.

Getting back to our study at hand, we need next look at the vowels accompanying the Name. We have already established that the vowel markings for יהוה are not the original. These were apparently lost and have been substituted for. The first vowel is a *shva*, or verbal stop, that was placed apparently to keep the ignorant from attempting the obvious and errant pronunciation of the first syllable as *Yah* (which is the way most want to pronounce it today) from the fact that this form occurs by itself in scripture. This first pointing, as we shall see, and the *dagesh* (a syllabic stop) in the third letter (*vav*) may be the only ones that hadn't been lost, thus proving out the Masoretic warning.

The next most precise markings in the Hebrew text are the accents. Experts in the specialized field of the *te'amim* observe that most variants are found in the Psalms, Proverbs, and Job, or the "Psalmodic" system. This system by its nature lends itself more to scribal change. The prosodic system used for the other books is much less forgiving in its relation to the grammar. There is no historical or grammatical reason to suspect the uses of these accents with regard to the Name.

There is no manuscript evidence either, to doubt the consonantal representations of the Tetragrammaton.[1] There is a minor pronunciation issue here, however. In ancient times, the sixth letter (*vav*) of the Hebrew alphabet, was enunciated like our "w." In modern usage, or Israeli Hebrew, it becomes a "v" sound. Additionally, the issue of which syllable receives the stress or accent is an important one. The entire meaning of a word may be changed simply with the change of emphasis from one syllable to the next.

Typically, the last syllable is stressed in Hebrew.[2] The vowel markings normally help indicate the emphasis; however, these being absent, we shall have to look elsewhere. Here again the melodies shed important light.

The most telling musical accent that accompanies the Tetragrammaton in scripture is called the *tsinnorit* (tube), or *tsinnor* if occurring at the end of a word. "As a rule it is marked on an open syllable immediately before the stress syllable."[3] Note that this fact alone rules out יהוה as being a two-syllable word such as *Yahweh*. The *Yah*, where the accent would have to fall, is a closed syllable, as in Psalm 96:10. The Name *must therefore be three and not two syllables*. From the standpoint of biblical numerology, we might also observe that the four consonantal letters plus the three syllables give us seven, the number of divine completion.

---

[1] The Essene writers of the Dead Sea Scolls used the modern block form of Hebrew except when writing the Tetragrammaton where they opted for the older Phoenician script form.

[2] Menahem Mansoor, Contemporary Hebrew 1, Behrman House, Inc. 1977. p.32

[3] Israel Yeivin, *Introduction to the Tiberian Masorah*, Scholars Press, 1980, p.273.

Music, Spirit, and the Keys to Prophecy

Fig. 6- Tsinnorit (encircled) with melodic rendering.
From Psalm 23. Editions Choudens, pg.1. S.H. Vantoura

The now discontinued grammar book entitled *201 Hebrew Verbs*, contains something of great interest to our study. The verb היה *hayah* or "to be", when contracted in the *Pi`el* and *Pu`al* (intensive) forms contains the consonantal form of the Tetragrammaton! The Hebrew grammarians, possibly by accident, worked out the lost pronunciation of God's name in accordance with all the known rules of Hebrew grammar. This occurs in the third-person masculine, future tense (modern Hebrew) or imperfect state (biblical Hebrew). (As opposed to modern Israeli Hebrew, the biblical verbs do not indicate the time of the action, only the state. Imperfect state means the action is not complete.)

Pi'el

III – הָוָה – הַוֵּה to form, to constitute: הַוֹּת, הַוֵּה

Past		Future		Present	Imperative	Gerund
הִוֵּיתִי	הִוִּינוּ	אֲהַוֶּה	נְהַוֶּה	מְהַוֶּה	הַוֵּה	בְּהַוֹּת
הִוֵּיתָ	הִוִּיתֶם	תְּהַוֶּה	תְּהַוּוּ	מְהַוָּה	הַוִּי	כְּהַוֹּת
הִוֵּית	הִוִּיתֶן	תְּהַוִּי	תְּהַוֶּינָה	מְהַוִּים	הַוּוּ	לְהַוֹּת
הִוָּה	הִוּוּ	יְהַוֶּה	יְהַוּוּ	מְהַוֹּת	הַוֶּינָה	מֵהַוֹּת
הִוְּתָה		תְּהַוֶּה	תְּהַוֶּינָה			

Pu'al

IV – הֻוָּה – הֻוָּה to be formed, to be constituted: הֻוֹּה

Past		Future		Present
הֻוֵּיתִי	הֻוֵּינוּ	אֲהֻוֶּה	נְהֻוֶּה	מְהֻוֶּה
הֻוֵּיתָ	הֻוֵּיתֶם	תְּהֻוֶּה	תְּהֻוּוּ	מְהֻוָּה
הֻוֵּית	הֻוֵּיתֶן	תְּהֻוִּי	תְּהֻוֶּינָה	מְהֻוִּים
הֻוָּה	הֻוּוּ	יְהֻוֶּה	יְהֻוּוּ	מְהֻוֹּת
הֻוְּתָה		תְּהֻוֶּה	תְּהֻוֶּינָה	

Fig. 7- The Name of God as it Appears in Hebrew Grammar Chart (removed from the current editions).
Abraham S. Halkin, Ph.D., *201 Hebrew Verbs* (Barron's Educational Series Inc., 1970) p.66.

With the vowel markings that are added here, we have the ineffable Name pronounceable in accordance with all the historical and grammatical rules of Hebrew. The mystical Tetragrammaton then re-emerges as *Yehaweh* (biblical) or *Yehaveh* (modern Israeli). (The passive *Pu'al* verb form does not fit the biblical description of the Creator and therefore is not a candidate.) The accent is appropriately on the last syllable, and the word has the necessary three syllables to accommodate the written musical accents used with it throughout the scriptures. The *sheva* is maintained under the first consonant (as well as the *dagesh* in the vav) indicating that the Masoretes likely knew of the syllabic divisions for the Name when publishing their texts.

"Yehaweh"
Fig. 8- The Name with vowel markings restored.

This restored pronunciation also harmonizes with the view of the first century historian Flavius Josephus. Being adamant that the Name was made up of four vowels, he spelled it out with Greek letters equating to IAUE.[1] As "h" is an open sound and is often treated as a vowel (arguably preceded by the preposition "an" in English usage), this suggestive, albeit imprecise rendering in the Greek may agree with the modern grammarian's reconstruction as well, however, such would not be a necessary support to our thesis.

Roughly translating the word we have, "He shall form, and continue to form." It is interesting to note that the replacement volume, *501 Hebrew Verbs* is *missing* these verb forms and therefore the Tetragrammaton itself. It appears that the grammarians realized what had occurred in their working out of the verb forms for "to be" and chose in retrospect to omit those that contained God's Name from the subsequent editions. This appears to be symbolic of the fact that the spiritual restoration of Israel is yet in the future (Jer.16:21, 23:27, Hos.2:17).

---

[1] Koster, C.J. *Come Out of Her My People,* Institute for Scriptural Research, South Africa, 1996, p. 132.

The many amateurish and dogmatic attempts seen previously seem to strengthen the ancient practice of secreting away the sacred markings in order to avoid their being *profaned* (or made common) by the uneducated and careless practitioner. Any rendering that does not account for the poetic nature of the biblical text, by observing all the known grammatical features of Hebrew, seems to run the risk of 'making common' the name of God and therefore, in this author's opinion, should be avoided. At best, the mispronunciations of God's name that seem designed to display its user's Hebraic knowledge, actually serve more to demonstrate one's ignorance of the same subject, as well an implied disdain for the work of the Masoretes.

Is the rendering contained herein, then, the Tetragrammaton revealed? Each must decide for himself. This restoration by the ever-punctilious Hebrew grammarians uniquely meets all the *linguistic, grammatical, historical,* and importantly, *melodic* requirements for the Name. As these verb forms were inexplicably deleted from the subsequent Hebrew grammar texts, this chapter also contains the only representations of the restored charts, and the now pronounceable name, currently in print.

9
Music and the End Times

Having laid a foundation for the art of music and the spiritual life from scripture and history, we may now make some new and exciting observations regarding the prophetic scriptures relating to the end-time events that precede the return of Christ to the earth.

Torah Types

The events described in the Torah relative to Israel are to be "ensamples," or divine imprints for the church (1 Cor. 10:11). The Greek word, *tupos,* most literally translates, "to deliver a blow" or "to strike." It creates the image of something that leaves a forceful impression. Those who maintain the view that the Torah is somehow no longer relevant instruction for the people of God are not sufficiently studied in either Old or New Testament doctrine.[1] (It is ironic that the very evangelical churches that resist using Old Testament scriptures with regard to holy living, quote from it liberally in reference to the tithe. In fact, more teaching on the righteous law of God would facilitate the kinds of blessings that could produce a healthier tithe.)

The events relative to Israel prior to the Exodus from Egypt may be considered a 'type' for the church prior to their deliverance from Mystery Babylon and the powers of this world at the end of the age. As we have seen, the musical liturgy for Israel was ordained prior to the Exodus "for a testimony." With the return of Christ at the conclusion of the Tribulation, a new priesthood and a new musical liturgy is established for the Sabbath Millennium and possibly for the Eternal State (Rev. 14:1-3). This liturgy includes once again instrumental music (harps), likely the ancient music tradition (song of Moses), and the *song of the Lamb* (Rev. 15:3). A 'new song' is also mentioned (Rev. 14:3).

When will this new music be learned? Will it be ordained prior to the church and Israel's Exodus from Mystery Babylon, as the Torah's pattern would indicate? I think this is a compelling question in the light of the restoration and correction referenced in this book and the recovery of the understanding of the biblical music.

The *song of Moses* will undoubtedly involve the literal restoration of the scriptures, i.e., in Hebrew, with the

---

[1] There are any of a number of books that are now available and quite comprehensive on this subject.

melody. It is the singing of the actual song from Exodus (15:1) that would be the most literal fulfillment.

Scripture tells of the restoration of a pure language in the context of the Millennial Kingdom (Zeph. 3:9). As something that has not previously existed cannot be restored, the most likely candidate for this fulfillment is the Hebrew language. Not only is it the language used by Moses and the prophets, but it also is said to have pre-existed even the Creation by ancient Rabbis.

Since the founding of the secular state of Israel, we have witnessed an unprecedented re-emergence of the long dormant language (although it also was considered as one of the chief candidates for the official language of the United States at its founding). The current revival of Hebrew should not be confused with the prophetic biblical fulfillment as many theologians today assert, but as a foreshadowing of a yet future event. Errors are made quite often concerning the modern state of Israel and the prophecies that, in context, should lead our expectations to the Second Coming and the Millennial Kingdom, not the necessary *worldly* precursors to those events, of which the secular state of Israel is one.

In addition to the restoration of the Hebrew language (Zeph. 3:9) for the Millenial Kingdom, we may also look for the restored prophetic ministry of song that accompanies the scriptures, so that they will again be heard in their fullest sense. I have observed to date, a powerful evangelizing effect from this use of this music; how much more will the Millennial ministry then carry the everlasting gospel?

Three Exoduses

The Apocalypse mentions three 'exoduses' of God's people from end-time Mystery Babylon. The first exodus is of the 144,000 Israelite witnesses and the saints at the en of the sixth seal. *". . . Do not harm the earth, the sea, or the trees till we have sealed the servants of our God on their foreheads."* (Rev. 7:4). The first 'mark of God' given for protection was placed on Cain, who slew his righteous brother, Abel, and was 'driven out' of Eden to wander the earth (Gen. 4:14-15). The one hundred and forty-four thousand end-time evangelists, who likewise slew their righteous brother, *Y'shua* "whom they have pierced" (Zech. 12:10),[1] and have wandered the earth in their exile from the Promised Land, in repentance receive God's 'seal' for protection during their Tribulational ministry. They are then caught up as a first-fruits unto the Lord and are pictured with Him on Mount Zion at His return.

"Then one of the elders answered, saying to me, "Who are these arrayed in white robes, and where did they come from?" And I said to him, 'These are the ones who come out of the Great Tribulation, and washed their robes and made them white in the blood of the Lamb.'" (Rev. 7:13-14). The saints are those persecuted and apparently martyred in the Great Tribulation and are seen worshiping before the throne of God in Heaven.

The second 'exodus' occurs with the rapture of the church and believing Israel with the seventh trumpet (at the end of the Tribulation) (1Cor. 15:52, Rev. 11:15). One third of the nation of Israel survives to be raptured with the remaining church (who hadn't yet died or been martyred) at the Lord's

---

[1] This typology helps identify the 144,000 as being physical Israelites only and should not be used to support Anti-Semitism, as it was the sins of all mankind that ultimately crucified Christ.

post Tribulational return. Here is when "all Israel" shall be believe and be saved (Rom.11:26). This precedes the pouring out of the bowls of wrath on the wicked.

The last 'exodus' will occur after the last bowl of wrath (plague) is poured out on Mystery Babylon under the seventh trumpet (Rev. 16:19). The bowls are a general replay of the plagues that the Lord inflicted on Pharaoh in ancient Egypt. Those who were unbelievers during the Tribulation and who also presumably did not take the "mark of the beast," were not raptured[1] at the sound of the seventh trumpet and are yet captives of Mystery Babylon at the Lord's return. The bowls of wrath will precipitate their release as the plagues on Egypt caused Pharaoh to release captive Israel in ancient times.

At the subsequent judgment of the sheep and the goats, those of this remaining group who fed, clothed, and visited the Lord's brothers (Israel and the church) during their Tribulational affliction (Matt. 25:34, 40), will be allowed to enter the Millennial Kingdom and populate the earth for a thousand years, thus completing this third and final exodus prior to the millennial government. (Many use this scripture as a call to minister the gospel to prisoners in general. Yet, in context the Lord specifically uses the term "brother" which always refers to those of the household of faith, Israel and the Church, not the truly lawless. They should receive the *just* execution of judgment in hopes of turning them to the gospel and of being an example to others.) It is the saints from the Tribulation period that will then rule with Christ for one thousand years as He sets up His government on earth (Rev. 20:4), restoring Israel to her glory and reigning from His throne in Jerusalem.

---

[1] Rapture is from the Latin. The Greek term is "harpadzo," and means to snatch or catch away, conveying the idea of a sudden force being excersized.

The Two Witnesses

The New Testament tells us that some time prior to the return of Jesus Christ to the earth, near the mid-point of the Tribulation, two individuals will rise up and begin to prophesy in the streets of Jerusalem to Israel and the nations (Rev 11:3). These two witnesses will display miraculous power and be protected from harm during the 42 months of their testimony. Most scholars believe that they will be Old Testament prophets, likely Moses and Elijah. This is credible from a number of angles. Given the state of modern religious compromise, it is unlikely that anyone from our generation is fit for a miraculous power such as these two figures will display.

"And if anyone wants to harm them, fire proceeds from their mouth and devours their enemies . . . These have power to shut heaven, so that no rain falls in the days of their prophecy; and they have power over waters to turn them to blood, and to strike the earth with all plagues, as often as they desire" (Rev.11:5-6).

Also, it was Moses and Elijah who appeared with Jesus on the Mount of Transfiguration (Matt.17:4), perhaps foreshadowing their Tribulational roles.

Given that the Two Witnesses are Old Testament saints, we now know that they will also be musicians, versed in the biblical notations. With the restoration of the Hebrew language in the nation of Israel, and the efforts of this ministry and others, the ancient biblical music is now beginning to spread to the evangelistic efforts there. What I first speculated a year ago, now appears to be a plausible scenario: that the Two Witnesses will prophesy to Israel in song, using the same melodies and language that they did in ancient times.

Given the confusion that has been interjected as to what the biblical faith is, through Christian misrepresentations as well as the Talmudic/rabbinic alterations, it is appropriate that God will use the two Old Testament prophets to sing the Bible clearly to Israel in the end-times. Also, even though the ancient notation has now been recovered, such that one today may ultimately learn it, it is highly unlikely that anyone from this generation could master this art with the short time that is left. The general public apathy as well as the rejection of this restored art by Orthodox Judaism, those with the most mastery of the Hebrew text, compounds the dilemma. Credible rumors are also circulating that government intelligence is beginning to target those with knowledge of the Hebrew syntax, perhaps hoping to thwart the prophecies. (This author has experienced the monitoring of his web-address on the part of government entities after only a few radio programs on Hebraic music). The only solution is apparently to send the two ancient prophets, who will not be corrupted or thwarted from delivering the full Bible message during the Great Tribulation.

Further evidence that the Two Witnesses will be musicians is found in the Bible in numerical typology. The number of musicians that were instructed in the "songs of the Lord" in the Davidic priesthood and later in the second temple was 288 (1Chron 25:7-31). As twelve is the number of divine government, 144 (12x12) is the number of God's *perfect witness*. (The number 144,000 represents, perhaps by way of a literal enumeration, the Israelite witnesses during the Great Tribulation [Rev. 7:1-6]. The New Jerusalem measures 144 cubits in height [Rev. 21:17]). *144 times 2 equals 288*, or two *perfect* witnesses. Thus the number of musicians instructed in the 'songs of the LORD' gives a prophetic foreshadowing of the Two Witnesses, connecting them directly to the music ministry and song. It may be that they will provide the ultimate proof of the musicality of the Bible.

These will of course be two individuals, not *groups* of people, such as the Church and Israel. This is indicated by the fact that their bodies will lie in the streets of Jerusalem for three and one-half days (Rev. 11:9), and that they are called "two prophets" (Rev. 11:10). They will be the first then to be resurrected at the end of the Tribulation Period.

Will the Two Witnesses thus prophesy to Israel in song? Will they use ancient instruments, or continue the biblical tradition of advancing the musical language (as is seen in the development of melody throughout the Bible) and use modern instruments? If opting for the ancient expressions, it is interesting to note that there are now instrument makers in Israel who research and recreate the ancient models. The fact that they will torment the *nations* with their prophesying indicates that they will likely use modern languages, possibly English as well as their native Hebrew tongue. Whatever the case may be, time will ultimately tell.

Once again, the Israelite nation will clearly hear the words of scripture and be given the clear choice to obey God's will, or not, as was the case in ancient times when the law was read to them.

"Then he took the Book of the Covenant and read in the hearing of the people. And they said, "All that the LORD has said we will do, and be obedient." (Exod. 24:7)

The 7th Trumpet and the Word of God

As was alluded to earlier, there is a consistency of imagery in the use of the trumpet call from Genesis to the

Revelation. Specifically, the te`amim indicate a rising fifth interval prior to each pronouncement that God makes in the Creation narrative (see Appendix 1). Israel was likewise commanded to blow the trumpet for the New Moon, (Psalm 81:3), the New Year, and the Year of Jubilee. In the case of the New Moon came the proclamation, "it is *sanctified*." [1] The seventh trumpet of Revelation is thereby blown (by the "mighty angel"), to signify the beginning of the Sabbath Millenium and its sanctification.

This consistency is most notable. Not only does the trumpet call always precede the Word of the Lord, but it also sanctifies what follows, e.g., the acts of Creation, the new month, and the Millennial Reign. It also is a call to worship.

The rising fifth interval is particularly fit for its biblical role, as it is the primary 'pure' interval within the musical scale, signifying not only God's holiness, but also having a symbolic purifying effect on what ever follows it. It is also the chosen musical cue that scripture gives us to announce the start of the Sabbath Millennium, *sounding* for a number of days.

The New Song

Sometime after the middle of the Tribulation, an elite group of evangelists are pictured with Christ on Mount Zion singing a "new song." This imagery suggests some interesting possibilities in our study of end-time music

The music is being taught by a group of harpists who are heard from heaven, "And they sang as it were a new song before the throne, before the four living creatures, and the elders; and no one could learn that song except the

---

[1] Eidersheim, Alfred. *The Temple* Mass. Hendrickson Publishers Inc, 1994. pg.229

hundred and forty-four thousand who were redeemed from the earth" (Rev 14:3). From the context, this appears to be a post-Tribulational event. They already have God's name "written on their foreheads," Christ is on the earth, and the angels are preparing for the bowl judgments, which follow the seventh trumpet. Additionally, their redemption from the earth is stated in the *past tense*.

(Characteristic to our time, there are those claiming to have already 'divined' this song by way of a mystical 'formula' found encoded in the Torah. Among other things, such a claim is totally out of the context of these scriptures which indicate the new song will be taught *from heaven*, and likely *after* the Second Advent.)

As prophetic revelation historically was presented to Israel in song form, (hence the early church's fondness for alluding to Christ as the "New Song"), these references likely point to aspects of a new doctrine or covenant that only the 144,000 sealed Israelites may learn and transmit. This would have to be the pure gospel of Christ (untainted by alterations accumulated through history) that leads the world in the Millennial Reign. The descriptions listed for its Israelite messengers are 1) purity, "not defiled by women", *spiritual* virgins as the marriage bed is undefiled (Heb.13:4), 2) fidelity "they follow the Lamb wherever He goes", and 3) honesty "and in their mouths was found no guile."

Beyond the historical references to the person and doctrine of Christ, the new song may have a more literal meaning. It may be that the Greek New Testament, having not been put to specific music, as were the Hebrew Scriptures, will be treated as such. It may be that a Hebrew version of this same text will be used with *te'amim* added. This would harmonize with the idea that the Hebrew language will be fully restored for the Millennial Kingdom. Perhaps, as with the inspired Hebraic music (chapters 3, 5), a specific modal structure will be utilized with the added feature of resolving to the 'octave above,' which is symbolic of the spiritual elevation available through Christ. It may also be that a song will be added that has not yet been presented.

Another group of harpers, those who have the victory over 'the beast', sing the song of Moses (probably being knowledgeable of the *te'amim*) and the song of the Lamb in preparation for the bowl judgments (Rev.15:2). This would have to be the saints that were martyred in the Tribulation or raptured at the seventh trumpet. The lyrics to the latter song are recorded in v. 3.

During the Millennial Kingdom the earth will be reverted to a restored state, where the lion lies down with the lamb. This may have implications for music as well. As acoustical physicists and studied musicians are aware, the modern musical scale has been slightly 'tempered' (detuned)[1] in order to facilitate the use of modulations of key and for ensemble playing (fretted instruments playing with voice for example). In this way we have become accustomed to hearing music that is not fully 'in tune.'

A situation analogous to that in sound is found in 'sacred geometry.' In this study asserts that a prime geometric building block of creation is found in the 'golden ratio of phi.' This phenomenon where the "ratio of the whole to the larger portion is equal to the ratio of the larger to the smaller portion" is evidenced in the proportions of various extremities of the human body to each other (forearms to hands, to fingers) as well as those of trees

---

[1] The original biblical music is best suited for purer 'Pythagorean' tuning, where the intervals are corrected to 'perfect' intervals.

(trunks to limbs to branches, etc.). The crux of the argument is that in using the pure ratios one may construct what appear as 'perfectly' shaped trees, yet when the ratios are slightly varied (representing 'the Fall') more natural looking trees are produced. Our tempered scale is a like scenario.

The new song may then involve the use of a 'corrected' harmonics that, while still based on our known system of seven, contains 'tuned' intervals. Or, there may be a new and unknown harmonic system altogether. With unlimited creativity as the governing factor, the possibilities are exciting to say the least!

A Restored Liturgy

We have learned thus far that a sacred liturgy has been foundational in God's plan from the beginning. The Old Testament is itself a musical liturgy, something that the early church likely maintained. Each reformation brought with it an art of musical worship. Gregorian chant, likely inspired by the Temple hymnody, blossomed in the Middle Ages. For his Protestant reformation, Martin Luther labored to create a fitting musical liturgy, even composing some of the songs himself, and eventually gleaning the inspiration of composers like J.S. Bach.

The predominantly gentile, western classical tradition, which dominated music for centuries, had played itself out by the end of the nineteenth century, turning into the chaotic forms of atonality and twelve-tone music. The best art music in the twentieth century was distinctively black (African American), through the dominance of the creative jazz and blues idioms, and then ethnic with a variety of folk idioms coming to the fore. The future of musical worship according to Bible prophecy, however, will be characterized by a strong Jewish influence.

We see in the Revelation that a sacred liturgy is preeminent among God's priorities in the Tribulation Period. If our typology proves correct, then the Two Witnesses will begin restoring the ancient Hebrew liturgy with their prophesying during the Great Tribulation (Rev. 11:3). The 144,000 evangelists will minister a 'new song,' and the overcoming saints will sing the song of Moses, and the song of the Lamb (Rev.15:3). Additionally, the music of Mystery Babylon will cease and the Jerusalem Temple worship will be restored, thus setting the overall tone for the Millennial Kingdom. As in ancient worship, the Word of God will be married to an artistic form of music. The simplistic and largely amateur folk/rock styles so dominant in the church today, will at best take a back seat, and God will once again be glorified by the best of our musical endeavors.

Isaiah wrote "They shall beat their swords into plowshares and their spears (*chanith*) into pruning hooks (*mazmorot*)" (Isa. 2:4), apparently describing a largely agricultural setting for the Millennial Kingdom of Christ. A closer look at the passage proves more revealing, however. The Hebrew word for spear, *chanith*, is synonymous to the singular noun *Cain*. The root, *koon*, translates to "a chant or mournful lament." The Hebrew word translated as pruning hook may be traced to its verb root, *zamar* (Strong's #2168), meaning "to trim." The identical word (#2167) means "to strike," i.e. a musical instrument. The noun *zammar* then may translate to "psalmist" or "plucker."

It would not be incorrect therefore to render this phrase, "And they shall beat their swords into plowshares, And their *mournful chants* into *psalms of praise*," thus emphasizing the worshipful and joyous nature of the earth during the reign of the Messiah.

'Date-Setters' and Prophetic Truth

Currently the study of Eschatology, or end time events, has been somewhat discredited by the many careless prognosticators of biblical events in our time. The seriousness of this subject, however, is punctuated throughout the scriptures and the standards for those claiming speak for God in matters of prophecy are most strict. The Torah, for instance, proscribes the death penalty for anyone who speaks a "word from the Lord" that does not come to pass (Deut. 18:20-22).

Despite the abuses, God's word also warned that deceivers would be a part of the scenery prior to His return. We must therefore analyze the nature of these errors and attempt a better understanding of the prophecies of the Bible, *not* merely reject them on account of the man-made abuses.

One common error is seen in the setting of specific dates as a guide to understanding where we are in the prophetic timeline. While the desire to connect dates and events is quite natural, we must be cautious of such practices.

Apart from the extreme examples, who may be easily be categorized as false prophets, the date-setters share a common problem with the principles of prophetic interpretation. These are ones that have scriptural teachings completely *backwards* regarding prophetic events. In Bible prophecy *dates don't determine events*, as these would have you believe, but rather observable *events determine the dates*! This is clearly seen in the following examples:

- **Date:** Last seven years of history
- **Event:** Covenant between Israel and her enemies, strengthened by the AntiChrist (Dan. 9:27). This event may not be completely obvious, however.
- **Date:** Last three and one-half years of history.
- **Event:** Abomination of desolation, captivity of half of Jerusalem (Dan. 9:27, Mic. 4:9-11). These and other related events will be unmistakable.
- **Date:** The start of the seventh millennium,
- **Event:** The blowing of the Seventh Trumpet, rapture of the Church. (Rev. 8:5, 1 Cor. 15:52).

Additionally, the seven seals of the Apocalypse, generally considered to represent the seven years of the Tribulation respectively, are also described by observable events, not dates (see Rev. 6-8).

God would have been unnecessarily complicating matters in describing prophetic events with such imagery and pointing us away from specific time calculations had He ordained that a corrected prophetic calendar would be in place by the start of the Tribulation. Indeed, of the Second Coming He told us, "But of that day and hour no one knows, no, not even the angels of heaven, but My Father only." (Matt. 24:36)

Some are teaching that the start of the Tribulation and the new Millennium coincide. This confused view actually places the reign of the AntiChrist in the same period as the reign of Christ! Not only does this twist the teaching of scripture on the issue, but it also casts doubt on the sovereignty of the Almighty in implementing His clearly stated chronologies, i.e., a one thousand year reign of Christ *on earth* (not nine hundred and ninety-three.)

Another recent example of date-setting by Christians was seen in the events surrounding 'Y2K.' Prophecy 'experts' in droves were setting various dates throughout the year of 1999 trying to predict computer-related catastrophes, which were then connected to prophetic events. Once again, each date passed without the corresponding event occurring. The experts quietly retreated without explanation.

Oslo Possibilities

The pre-Tribulation rapture theory, which the evangelical church has embraced wholesale, has many scholars prematurely focusing on this event alone, thereby ignoring other indicators that may place us in the Tribulation period.

Additionally, many have embraced the "imminent return" doctrine, which states that the Second Coming can occur at any time, and therefore are not looking to understand the signs of the times. This view also contradicts the prophecies that give us clear signs and events to watch for, *leading up to* His return (see Matt. 24, Dan. 9, Revelation).

Another false view teaches that the first three and one half years of the Tribulation were fulfilled during Jesus' earthly ministry, which was perhaps roughly that length, ending with His crucifixion. A two thousand year gap has supposedly ensued and we need look only for the fulfillment of the last three and one-half years, or Great Tribulation. The problems with this view are several.

First, the apostle John wrote the seven seals Revelation after the death of Christ, to describe the events of the

Tribulation. From a consensus of scholars, as well as from the typology seen in the other biblical weeks, we know that the seals most likely summarize the respective years of the Tribulation. Also, all other biblical dramas that are constructed as a week have consistent lengths within the various 'days,' with the exception of the Creation Week. Even in this week, it is only the seventh day that is anomalous, as it is the open-ended Sabbath day of the Creator. The trumpet judgments, which are not necessarily time-specific, also contain a variation on the Sabbath, as it is the seventh trumpet that sounds for a period of days (Rev. 10:7). This, too, is symbolic of the Creation Week sabbath which has been several days long, i.e. over several thousand years long. A mid-week 'break' would also symbolically leave the Tribulational drama suspended, and unresolved, for an extended period of time on the discordant theme of the Crucifixion. This, too, is out of character of the master dramatist of the Bible who, as demonstrated in previous chapters, always resolves the mid-week discord in a timely and redemptive manner. This is a strong principle to observe, and one quite useful in correcting the many varied and creative inventions that have the presumption of inspired prophetic interpretation.

The proponents of this two-thousand year gap theory, are ultimately mixing and matching the dramas of two separate weeks, i.e. the first half of the Crucifixion week with the second half of the Tribulation week. This is simply more confusion masquerading as prophetic wisdom.

For these various reasons, most of the prophecy teachers of today have been overlooking the possibility that the covenant of Daniel, and therefore the start the Tribulation may have already been fulfilled through the Oslo process. The clearest scriptural signpost for the beginning of the

Tribulation is the covenant of Daniel 9:27, a false guarantee of peace between Israel and her enemies. "Then he shall confirm a covenant for one week . . ." This covenant would begin the last seven years of judgment on Israel and the corresponding Tribulation period, leading to the return of Christ.

The Wye River Accord of October 1998 (Oct. 19-23), made between Israel's Netanyahu, Yassar Arafat, and Bill Clinton, is the third in the series of Oslo peace agreements. It is also the last one of the three to remain a candidate to fulfill Bible prophecy as time and events have by now disqualified Oslo I and II (we have passed the three and one-half year mark for both and have not seen the corresponding events of the Great Tribulation occur). The peace process in Israel is also now on hold, being in serious failure since a renewed and sustained outbreak of violence between Israel and the Palestinians starting in late 1999.

As the strengthening of the covenant does not need to be apparent, and therefore does not necessitate one of its *public* supporters to be identifiable as the AntiChrist (he could be a figure working behind the scenes at this point), this too would place the current Wye accord as a candidate.

One other factor militates for the Wye accord. Biblical typology strongly indicates that Christ will return and literally fulfill the fall feasts. Just as His crucifixion precisely fulfilled the spring feasts (as discussed in chapter 3), Christ's return will complete the cycle with the fall feasts. This means that the covenant of Daniel would have to be made sometime in the autumn in order to place the return at the correct season, seven years later. The Wye River accord now uniquely fits this pre-requisite as well.

If then the Wye accord proves itself out as the covenant of Daniel, we will enter the Great Tribulation, which will be an unmistakable event to most, on or near April 1st (fools day) to the 4th, of 2002. Christ will then return approximately three and one half (prophetic, 360 day*) years later in a literal fulfillment of the Jewish fall feasts.

*(Thirty-day months are the biblical standard. The Genesis flood caused a collapsing of the water-vapor canopy, something that increased the rotation of the earth, thus creating 365 and 1/4 day, years. God, however, never went off the original 'prophetic' calendar. This is clearly seen in Revelation 11:3 and 12:6 where 1260 days is equal to three and one half years, (1260÷360=3.5). Any calculations of prophetic time must therefore be in conformity with twelve thirty-day months.)

The Mid-East violence has recently spread to previously untouched American soil with a horrific terror assault on the World Trade Center and the Pentagon. Islamic terrorists, acting in tandem, hijacked four commercial jetliners, crashing two into the respective twin towers of the World Trade Center in New York, and one into the military fortress of the Pentagon in Washington D.C. The fourth jet appeared headed for Camp David, the site of the Middle-East peace talks, before being thwarted by passenger heroics. Alerted to the hijacker's motives via cell-phones, some men on board overtook the hijackers, crashing in an unpopulated rural area in Pennsylvania.

As an ironic twist, the attack in New York took place on September 11, or "9-11", a date the initial Mid-East peace talks at Camp David occupied in 1978 as well as the emergency exchange number used to exhaustion that tragic day. The twin towers also stood in view as a large #11.

Iraq is suspected of instigating anthrax attacks in America and of involvement in the World Trade Center destruction. Saddam Hussein who is in the location of the historical king of the North has taken the title Nebuchadnezzar II out of his desire to take Israel into another captivity. Recent events currently have the short-term potential to bring the superpower United States into an all out confrontation with the Arab states, cripple its economy and plunge the world into the subsequent events of the Great Tribulation.

Secular intelligence experts are starting to pay close attention to this time frame as well. World Net Daily, in referencing Israeli intelligence gatherers, *Debka Files*, says the "next-most-likely timeframes for violence [in the Middle-East] are April, 2002, " and that the "violence could take the form of a wider regional war" in which the "implications could reach beyond the region."[1]

We should therefore watch diligently to see if these biblical events begin to take place at this time. They would include: the starting of Israelite animal sacrifices on a reconstructed alter which are then halted by the AntiChrist (Dan. 9:27), who then blasphemes God. The capture of half of Jerusalem by armies from the north (Micah 4:9-11), and believers fleeing to the mountains from Judea (Matt. 24:15-16). If these events and the related fulfillments of the first four seals of the Apocalypse do not transpire by the spring of 2002, then we must look to a yet future covenant to begin the Tribulation period and thus fulfill Daniel's prophecy.

The 'Musical' Apocalypse

In the rush to identify end-time characters and events, there has been a neglect of a significant aspect of the Apocalypse, that of its overall context and dramatic meaning. In short, the Revelation of John is, as the rest of scripture and Creation, a very detailed and *aesthetically* conceived drama. It is here that God addresses the cosmic themes of existence and *corrects* and *restores* all things to His divine order.

---

[1] *Trouble in the Holy Land,* by Jon Dougherty. World Net Daily.com 10/29/01.

The structure of the events also conforms precisely to the same devices that are operative within the physics of the musical scale. The Apocalypse is therefore musically and dramatically logical and consistent. What follows is an overview of this phenomenon.

The first seal (first year) strikes the tonic of the key and therefore gives a sense of the tonality for the entire piece. This theme has as its focus the nation of Israel and the theme of peace (Dan 9:27, Rev 6:1). The next two seals (years) correspond to the supertonic and mediant intervals and are intermediate dramatic devices. Here we see the status quo being challenged and the set-up for further drama. Under the second seal, it is granted to take the peace of the first seal from the earth. The third seal describes a state of inflation. (Rev. 6:3-4, 5-7). The fourth seal (or sub-dominant) and fifth seal (dominant) are more definitive and eventful as they are also musical cadence points (Rev. 7-8, 9-11). These include wars, famine and the martyrdom of believers. The non-scale tri-tone also occurs here (mid-scale) and is the most discordant interval in the scale, paralleling the theme of the Great Tribulation (mid-point). The focus is toward tests and trials on earth and spiritual purity as the musical 4th and 5th are the 'pure' intervals of the scale. The sixth-seal shifts focus to earthly dominion as God starts to state His claim in the earthly realm with great natural disruptions (Rev. 6:12-7:4). The sixth interval or *super-dominant* proceeds from the "dominant" fifth and is a rich and dramatic (or earthly) sounding device. The seventh seal, or leading-tone, is that which concludes the drama and leads to the final resolution at the octave (Rev. 8:1-9-21). This interval is characterized by suspense and an anticipation of its musical resolution. Here the trumpet judgments are sounded and earth is purified for the

Millennial Kingdom. After this the seventh trumpet sounds and declares the resolution of the Tribulation and the beginning of Christ's reign on earth (Rev. 11:15). This is the beginning of the eighth year, or musical octave. This signifies a return to the key center. The theme of peace that was stated at the beginning of the drama is now restated, but in a higher register. This is now not the false, worldly peace of the AntiChrist, but the refined and heavenly Peace of the true Christ now come to earth. Praise the LORD.

To summarize the function of the scale; the tonic sets the tone and key center, the second and third provide dramatic color, the fourth and fifth are pure intervals and points of temporary resolution, the sixth and seventh provide further transitional material, and the octave is a return to the key center in a *higher* register.

The Trumpet Judgments and Their 'Unisons'

The seven trumpet judgments (sounding during the seventh seal [or year] of the Apocalypse) also correlates thematically with the other weeks of scripture. Although not coinciding chronologically with the seven seals, because they fall under the seventh seal, the trumpets judgments speak to events and themes occurring respectively in all the other weeks of scripture. Recall that one of the functions of the trumpet-call in ancient Israel was to *warn of impending judgment*. The trumpet *judgments* under the seventh seal of the Apocalypse either *correct* or *restore* the various events that occurred in the preceding "sevens" of the Bible. In each case, they directly address the main thematic events of the corresponding days of the other weeks. The literary images therefore correspond to each other. The trumpet call also serves another historic function, of *calling for battle* (in the case of the seventh trumpet, Armageddon) and of sanctifying that which follows (the Millennial kingdom). In fact, all of the ancient uses of the trumpet calls are summarized here, including the *ceremonial* use (for the Wedding Feast of the Lamb). Notice also the use of *key words* and *literary images* linking the respective *days* of scripture, and the shifting of focus from *the heavenly realm to the earthly realm*. The drama is overall one of *bringing the heavenly realities to earth* in an orderly fashion and through multiple stages of development.

1st Trumpet Rev. 8:7 This sets the thematic center which the drama will work from and return to. It is the start of the trumpet judgments and the sanctifying of *the earth* for the return of Christ. *Trees and green grass* (false gods of *earth* worship) are burned up, one third.
-Day 1-
Creation week: The heavens and *earth* and night and day are created on the first day, the setting for subsequent events of week.

Crucifixion Week: This day is characterized by branches of palm *trees* greeting Jesus' entry to Jerusalem (John 12:12) and by cries of "Peace in Heaven" (Luke 19:38).

Tribulation Week: Characterized by a crown (or wreath made of leaves of a *tree* as worn by Roman Emperors) being given (Rev. 6:2) and a Peace treaty (Dan. 9:27) with Israel and her enemies. (Peace is often characterized by an olive branch.)

2ⁿᵈ Trumpet Here the status quo is challenged. A great *burning mountain* cast into *the sea*. (Rev. 8:8). The Torah was given on *Mount* Sinai as the "LORD descended upon it *in fire*" (Ex 19:18). The sea is often typical of people. Here, perhaps the Torah is figuratively cast into the sea of people of the earth, to make them accountable to the Law of God and to *separate* them. A literal fulfillment may involve the real Mt. Sinai in Saudi Arabia. If so, we will see a flood engulf the recently discovered *Jabal Moussa* (whose top was literally burned by fire) as the second trumpet sounds.
-Day 2-

Creation week**:** God *separates* the *waters*.

Crucifixion Week: Christ curses fig tree (tree of the knowledge of good and evil)[1] and teaches that faith can cast *"mountain into the sea"* (Matt. 21:21). Judas given power to take Prince of *Peace* (Christ) from earth (Luke 22:5).

Tribulation Week: a sword given to take *peace* from the earth, that people should kill one another (i.e., waters separate).

3ʳᵈ Trumpet Rev. 8:10-11 Star (Lucifer Isa. 14:12) falls to earth and makes the *waters* (people?) bitter. People who were given a chance to receive God's Torah (2ⁿᵈ trumpet) fall prey to Lucifer and become bitter, many die. Literal fulfillment would involve poisoned water source.
-Day 3-

Creation Week: *waters are gathered* into "one place" (Gen. 1:9).

---

[1] As thought by ancient Rabbis. Martin, Ernest L. *Secrets of Golgotha*. Oregon: Associates for Scriptural Knowledge, 1996, p.385.

Crucifixion Week: people *gather* into the temple (one place) to hear Christ (Luke 22:38).

Tribulation: oil and wine (*liquid*, typical of believers, gather) cannot be harmed.

4th Trumpet Rev. 8:12 *Sun, moon, and stars* (false gods of the pagans) struck, (one third).

As the Lord was struck (one third of the Trinity) at the end of the fourth millennium of history, so shall these idols of the pagans be struck under this trumpet.

-Day 4-

Creation Week: *sun, moon, and stars* were created (Gen. 1:14-19).

Crucifixion Week: *Son* of God is "struck" and crucified (Matt. 27:26, John 19:31-37).

Tribulation Week: The Great Tribulation begins for Israel and believers. God's people are typified by the *moon* as they reflect the light of the Sun (Christ) and the twelve tribes of Israel are *stars* ("I will multiply your descendents as the stars of heaven" Gen. 22:17) and are represented by the zodiac. Both are *struck* by the ungodly Rev. 6:7.

5th Trumpet Rev. 9:1 Star (Christ, Morning Star) figuratively falls from heaven to earth, *given the keys* to the bottomless pit. *Creatures* are released to harm men who don't have God's seal. This trumpet represents *heavenly dominion* and purity.

-Day 5-

Creation Week: *Life* is created in the form of sea *creatures* and birds on earth (Gen. 1:20-23).

Crucifixion Week: Christ is put into the earth (*given keys* to death and hell). Eternal *life* is available to all who believe.

Tribulation Week: Martyrs under the alter of God (Rev 6:9), given white robes *(purity)* and told to *rest* (Rev. 6:11). They overcome death and Hell in their martyrdom, "not loving their lives until the end" (Rev. 12:11). The theme is spiritual or heavenly dominion, true *life*.

6th Trumpet Rev. 9:13. The sixth-day speaks to a *preparation for the sabbath* and, as seen in the Creation week, *dominion of the earthly* realm. With this trumpet four angels are released to kill a third of mankind with *fire, smoke and brimstone*. Seven thunders sound, yet are sealed up.[1] This is the final preparation for the Sabbath Millennium.

-Day 6-

Creation Week: Man and beast created, man given *dominion* over earth (Gen. 1:26).

Crucifixion Week: Christ's followers prepare spices and fragrant oils and *prepare* for the sabbath (Mark 16:1, Luke 23:56), Christ takes *dominion* over death and hell.

Week of History: Man subdues and *dominates* the earth during this millennium (approximately 1000-2000 A.D). The worldly powers of the nations, represented by heraldic 'beasts' (bear, lion, eagle, etc.) *dominate* the earth through

---

[1] Thunder as well as other natural phenomenon such as earthquakes are typical in the Bible of God's speaking (Ps.77:18, 104:7 Is. 29:6).

war and conquest. The Gospel is preached to all in preparation for the Sabbath Millennium.

Tribulation Week: This is the most eventful seal yet. It is under this seal that *dominion of the earth* is perceived as changing from the rulers of this world, to that of Christ. Key images are *fire, smoke and brimstone* and the *four angels*. The 144,000 Israelite servants are sealed as the four angels of the sixth trumpet judgment are told to wait.

Seventh Trumpet Rev. 11:15   This trumpet sounds to begin the Sabbath Millennium. As the Israelite priests blew the trumpet at the new moon and proclaimed "it is sanctified", so the Great High Priest blows this trumpet at the beginning of the Sabbath Millennium. Imagery includes *lightenings, thunderings, earthquakes, and noises*.

Creation Week: God rests from all His work, yet there are many *storms* on earth during human history.

Crucifixion Week: Christ's followers rest on the sabbath (Luke 23:56). Jesus resurrected with deceased saints (Matt 27:53) and there is an *earthquake* (Matt 27:50).

Seventh Seal of Tribulation Week: The angel throws censer to the earth with *noises, thunderings, lightnings, and an earthquake*. It is the final year of preparation for the Sabbath Millennium. The trumpet judgments are sounded during this seal, all to sanctify the following millennium of Christ's reign on earth. The resolution of the Tribulation starts after the seventh-trumpet sounds at what would be the eight year, or octave, placing all things back at the "tonic" but spiritually and literally in a "higher register" i.e. the Millennial Reign of Christ.

The seven bowls of wrath proceed from the seventh trumpet and are poured out on the wicked at the start of the Sabbath Millennium. These generally parallel the plagues on Egypt prior to the Exodus. This in type relates to those yet in bondage to Mystery Babylon that were not taken in the rapture at the seventh trumpet (1Cor. 15:52) but who will enter the Millennial Kingdom at the judgment of the sheep and the goats (Matt. 25:32-34). It is also a call to the battle at Armageddon and the Wedding Feast of the Lamb.

As the weeks of scripture and human history correlate to the trumpet judgments and the seals of the Apocalypse, they are also united thematically by key words and literary themes contained in each of their respective days. Far from being a series of disjointed and confusing events as many teachers throughout history have portrayed it, the Revelation is a precise summation and a culmination of the main themes of God's drama of the ages. Thus the Author of Creation displays His sovereign command over the dramatic elements of history and the Bible from the beginning to the end of time, and beyond.

For our generation, the dominant art form will not be music that is played on radios, CD players, in movie theatres or even concert halls. Instead, the irrepressible 'music' of our time will be the Tribulation Period itself, being played out upon the soundstage of the earth, concluding the current era of human history and ushering in the return of the Lord with the sound of the Great Shofar (trumpet) (1Cor. 15:52).

10

Modern Music: The Battlefield

Music of Mystery Babylon

Those of us who have lived through, or rather *survived* the latter half of the 20th Century, have witnessed what may only be referred to as the progressive debasement of our culture in general and of popular music specifically. By no means can this author be termed a musical 'prude', having an appreciation of most music styles of the day; however, we must address the willful debasement being seen in the modern culture.

What has been witnessed to date is anything but subtle. It has been the standard for some time now, that for a group or individual to be promoted and therefore to achieve success in the entertainment arena, a performer must, be willing to push the standards of decency and morality back a notch (or more). Talent has in the past been a helpful starting place, but now even that prerequisite is thrown out the window in what passes for popular entertainment today. Ultimately technology and mass media collaborate to produce an otherwise unimaginable effect, i.e., to make sin appear glamorous and God to seem boring!

A common phenomenon within the realm of popular entertainment mediums is that of a person, or group creating, or 'caught' in some scandalous affair. Soon after, they seem to acquire mainstream 'star' appeal, with all the attendant media and studio promotion. It is as if they have passed some sort of bizarre initiation and are therewith admitted into the entertainment 'club.' This oft-repeated chronology of events further begs the question of what is truly being sought in today's performers.

The use of something enjoyable (as is entertainment) to carry the worldly, and therefore satanic, message is no new strategy. Alcoholic beverages, for instance, are usually a blend of good, God-made ingredients combined or tainted with the toxic. The same may be said of foods today, which are loaded with chemicals and preservatives. It is the mixture of good elements with tainted ones in any realm that are often the most destructive. No one would drink poison undiluted, but alcoholic drinks kill millions each year with their deceptive blends. This same principle has been operative in music and the arts, from ancient times on. Greek literature records that one of the pagan Muses (hence, music) spoke to a Greek poet, saying, "We know how to tell many lies which are like the truth; we also know how to tell the truth when we wish . . ."

Going back just to the era of the forties and fifties and performers such as Frank Sinatra and Ella Fitzgerald, we have some very appealing forms of music with great and talented performers, yet corrupt ideals. The most prominent vices at this time were smoking, drinking, womanizing, and self-reliance.

The rock-n-roll invasion brought a debasement of another type. Musically derived from some appealing musical styles rooted in Negro spirituals, which became the blues, and developed into R&B, rock musicians adapted and corrupted the forms. The term, 'rock and roll,' is known to derive from a slang word for sexual intercourse. It was primarily an expression and glorification of the adolescent experience. Ultimately the music escalated cultural immorality with the promotion of illicit drugs, open sexual expressions, occultism, and a general theme of rebelliousness. The protests of previous generations fell on deaf ears largely due to the hypocrisy of their stand; if you don't truly repent of your own sins, it is futile trying to convince others—especially those of succeeding generations—of theirs.

The sixties revolt turned into the seventies materialism, and then the further degradation of the eighties, and nineties. The 'set' changes, but the governing principles remain the same; succeeding generations attempt to outdo the depravity of the last, only with a different 'style.'

The artistic quality of the music characteristically becomes worse, (compare Sinatra's music, which could legitimately be called an art, to that of any pop legend today, none of whom approach such a description), and the levels of human debasement escalate. One can easily imagine that cross-dressing Satanist Marilyn Manson or gangster rapper 'Snoop Doggy Dog' would have had a tough go of it in any previous era's musical culture.

We truly seem to be at a time when popular music can devolve little further without involving open sex and human sacrifice, likely to a tribal drum beat, on the public stage. In actuality, native drumming is now the rave amongst the culturally 'hip,' and *enactments* of sex and sacrifice are occurring on the concert stage. It frightfully appears to be only a matter of time until these expressions, too, are fully realized.

Writing in the context of the music of Mystery (or hidden) Babylon, the prophet John states, "by your *sorcery* all the nations were deceived" (ital. added Rev 18:22-23). The Greek word for sorcery is *pharmakeia* (Strong's #5331) from which we get our word pharmacy. This appears to point directly to our time and the use of drugs, legal and illegal, their deceptive influence, as well as the use of music to promote them.

The Message of the Medium

Successful pop stars may be identified by the particular societal and moral boundaries that they were able to break down. In the case of the Beatles, it was the introduction of drugs, sexual immorality, rebellion to authority, occult religions, and the like within the American mainstream culture. John Lennon and Paul McCartney, now musical and cultural icons, were only common club musicians before being 'discovered.' Their phenomenal success was due in no small part to their being surrounded by the best talent in the recording industry, the use of the then new multi-track recording technology, and the excessive media exposure that was given to their work.

The true significance of the Beatles, from the historical perspective, seems to be a proving out of the idea that having a rare talent would no longer be requisite for success in the arts. Media and technology could now combine to make the person with an *average talent* a 'star.' (It well known that today's producer, more than the artist, is the staple of the recording industry). Having this type of control meant that the recording industry could raise up anyone that would carry its corrupt messages, no longer needing to be subject to the inconveniences of studied artists, who are more likely to possess an innate integrity, (and a good bit of temperament to boot). Rock thereby became the vehicle through which moral and cultural debasement could accelerate like never before. This occurrence, more than any other within the pop culture, in this author's opinion, was truly symbolic of "the day the music died."

The entertainment media's anti-God bias is becoming more and more apparent. In polling the public as to the best song of the twentieth century, the major media overwhelmingly proclaimed the winner to be *Imagine* by John Lennon. A recent B.B.C. News 'poll' has declared it no less than the second favorite song *of all time.* While an independent public polling would hardly place this sparse ballad with such prominence, a quick look at the lyrics is most revealing:

"Imagine there's *no Heaven*, it's easy if you try. No Hell below us, above us only sky—You may say I'm a dreamer, but I'm not the only one. I hope one day you'll join *us*, and the world will be as *one*."

The song is, in effect, an anthem for 'imagining' a one-world government under the AntiChrist, (which is the only true option to biblical Christianity). This is a dream that Bible prophecy warns about and one that appears to be popular amongst the media and Hollywood elite.

It is certain, from the biblical perspective, that Mr. Lennon's *imagination* alone was not sufficient as he went into eternity and stood before his Creator and ultimate Judge for, "All have sinned and fall short of the glory of God" (Rom. 3:23). Hopefully, he was granted repentance prior to this event.

The pop superstar, Madonna, was a skilled promoter to adolescent girls of the idea that it was 'cool' to be sexually loose, something that females were neither culturally, nor are by nature, inclined to be. Her work as a pop icon has been seen even to cross line of the pornographic.[1] Songstresses of the past, in performing a higher quality of material, thereby also needed better-trained voices to advance their careers, not mere sexual and cultural 'shock appeal.'

(Analyses of this type always elicit the question, "but don't you like their songs?" While I must answer "yes" to limited amounts of these entertainers material, the destructive messages far outweigh any pleasure derived from their music).

Much has been made of the fact that Madonna is the product of a traditional Catholic background, as though it is somehow anomalous with her career. Nothing could be further from the truth. This religion has been unusually adept at misrepresenting the Christian faith to biblically illiterate people throughout history,[2] and the result, as seen here, is often most tragic. Those who have been injured by religious misrepresentations of God, often become just such anti-heroic figures. As punctuation to this perceived irony,

---

[1] Her 1992 pictographic book, "Sex," easily fits this category, as do arguably many of her performances.
[2] A confused blend of pagan traditions with biblical morality, the Catholic religion has admittedly also produced worthy spiritual scholarship through the ages.

Madonna recently married filmmaker Guy Ritchie, who is a descendant of a 'canonized' Jesuit priest, Sir John Ogelvie. She also appears to be pursuing some sort of status with European royalty, and has sought papal blessing for her son.[1] As with many pop stars that become successful on the platform of rebelliousness to society, her true ambition appears to be that of becoming part of the establishment elite, on the backs of her many gullible fans, of course.

Esoteric religions have now become 'center stage' by way of the world's entertainment mediums. The major stars of today boast of spiritual beliefs such as Scientology, Buddhism, New Age, Cabbala, Atheism, and the like. (Of course, anyone maintaining a strong Christian testimony is virtually left out of the equation). New Age[2] references are particularly cliché in today's song titles and lyrics. The concert sets and record logos of even the most mainstream of popular performers depict such things as pyramids (representing ancient Egyptian deities and worship), tail-swallowing serpents (or circles of reincarnation) and other such religious symbologies. Hollywood's 'Christian' stars, if they can be identified at all, are mostly that 'in name only,' expressing at best a vague and apologetic affiliation with the King of the universe.

The classical arts have followed, or even established, the same form. Though more cerebral in their approach, composers have come to a 'crises of means' in their expressions. Moving from tonal music to atonal at the turn of the twentieth century, to 12-tone and other increasingly

---

[1] Andrew Morton, *Madonna*. St. Martin's Press, 2001. 175 Fifth Avenue, New York, N.Y., p. 210, 230.
[2] "New Age," is now also a marketing term used to describe a musical style. From this book's perspective, the music itself is not necessarily corrupt, nor are its artists all practitioners of this religion.

chaotic expressions, modern composers have musically captured the nihilistic ideal of the meaningless existence.

The twentieth century is unique in accomplishing the total breakdown of the tonal system within the context of serious music (see chapter 4, Arnold Schoenberg and 12-tone music). As it is the tonal system that symbolically plays the themes of the Creation, history, and the Bible, such a breakdown musically represents the moral crisis that was prophesied to be in place prior to the return of Christ to the earth, where men will be "always learning and never able to come to the knowledge of the truth" (2Tim. 3:1-7).

The only refuge for anything approaching a biblical expression is found in Contemporary Christian Music (CCM). Yet this promising medium, too, has been compromised as the economic control has largely shifted to large secular corporations such as Sony Records. The music tends to deliver a watered-down gospel message, in styles that shout of compromise with the world, rather than the confrontation of it, and the pursuit of sales, not souls.

Bright spots may be found in jazz and other instrumental forms that by nature carry less overt messages of corruption. Stylistically, today, there is more variety available than ever, but the messages sadly remain exclusively secular.

Conversely, it is unfortunate that any artistic music is virtually banned from today's worship. The preponderance the simpler folk music expressions today seems to symbolize a church *relating to its Creator on the level of elementary to adolescent love*, as opposed to the more mature expressions seen in the scriptures (see chapter 6) and at other times in history. Hopefully the thoughts expressed in this book will help in countering this trend.

The Movies

Motion pictures today typically carry overt as well as subtle messages of corruption. Stories with plots about fallen angels mating with women (City of Angels), and aliens in messianic roles (E.T.), seem to closely mirror the Bible descriptions of demons. The main difference is that Hollywood today casts the demons in the role of hero.

One movie that passed under the radar due to its subtleties, was the popular movie, "The Truman Show," starring Jim Carrey. Advertised as being a story about someone that literally grew up in a television show, his life being the show, this movie appears more to be an allegory about rebelling against Christianity.

The plot revolves around the main character, Truman (*True-man*), coming to the realization that his entire life is a fabricated illusion. The show's director, who is named Cristoff (*Christ-off*), confronts Truman via the intercom (in a God-like 'voice from heaven') saying, "I am the *Creator* (pause) of a show that gives hope to the masses," he then urges him to continue participating in the 'show'. Truman chooses to pursue freedom rather than continue in the *illusion* of Cristoff and attempts to 'leave the set' (a small town). Storms are created to dissuade his leaving (symbolic of the Tribulational judgments?). One scene shows the hero, appearing dead, with outstretched arms and a rope on his body in the sign of a cross (mock crucifixion). He revives (mock resurrection) to reach the end of the 'set' and a staircase leading to an exit. The plot resolves as Truman climbs the staircase, (or 'works,' steps of freemasonry), and exits the false reality of the Creator, to the cheers of the viewing masses.

The heroes and heroines of today's dramas are predominantly cast as secular, and even overtly occult characters. This is now carried to the extent of pushing the practice of sorcery on children through the "Harry Potter" books and movies. Compromised Christian and conservative leaders such as Focus on the Family, and film critic Michael Medved, failed to condemn this cultural heresy at the outset, giving such rationale as, "at least the kids are reading again." A children's version of the Satanic Bible must therefore be an acceptable idea to such supposed cultural reformers, as long as it is done in an entertaining and "clean" fashion.

Of course, it is also now fashionable to cast the villains of today's dramas as being religious, specifically biblical/Christian characters. Recent movies such as Cape Fear, A Few Good Men, and The Rapture, seem to portray that fundamental Christianity is akin to a homicidal pathology. Anymore it is rare that a person of faith is given any depth of character, let alone cast as the hero.[1] It is a poignant testimony that such a complete cultural reversal was accomplished in just the last half of the twentieth century.

Throughout history, occult and 'New Age' theology (an old idea) has taught that there will be a time when man will throw off the restraints of Christianity, (represented in the Zodiac by Pisces the fish), and enter a new (Aquarian) age of en*light*enment. (Note also that the name Lucifer means "light-bearer"). This is actually a mimicry of the biblical millennium of Christ. The same lie from the Garden—that man can become as God (Gen. 3:5), is thereby being taught and is gaining much popularity today. Many preachers are now describing America as a "post-Christian" society. Be

---

[1] A notable exception is the independently written and produced movie of 1988, "The Apostle," by Robert Duvall.

assured, however, there is no *post-Christian* society mentioned in the Bible, only *pre-Judgment*!

"... *If you do not obey the voice of the LORD your God, to observe carefully all His commandments which I command you today, that all these curses will come upon you and overtake you* ..." (Deut. 28:15).

The Road to Redemption

Each must find in his own heart where he participates in any societal decline, but I shall name a few obvious categories, though in no particular order:

-Musicians have sold out for the lure of success. From the obvious cases such as the Rolling Stones (whose recent 'Bridges to Babylon' tour alone earns them entry into this section, notwithstanding the fruits of their entire career), to the more neutral pop artists of today, few indeed have wholeheartedly applied their talents to serve and glorify their Creator. In fact, the gross disproportion in those of mediocre talent receiving such extraordinary compensation ultimately speaks to the selling of souls (the performer's and their audience's) rather than abilities. Recall that Satan tempted Christ by offering Him the 'kingdoms of the world' if He would fall down and worship him (Matt. 4:8-9). The adversary was not rebuked for making a false offer and still has the ability to bestow such worldly rewards on those who will serve his corrupt cause.

Something that increasing numbers of popular musicians today would thereby do well to consider, is the fact that 'hell,' as biblically described, is a literal place with differing levels of torment. Those who lead others to death and depravity for commercial success are sure to qualify for an unpleasant eternity short of true repentance.

Certainly, the pop music lifestyle leads to death, if anyone is minimally honest about the subject.

-Each generation who has been unrepentant of their own compromise, by supporting their favorites from the 'good old days,' and even holding on to relics of musical and moral corruption, must be named. Even many Bible believers won't let go of the likes of old rock and roll favorites, despite the obvious non-Christian messages (an analysis of popular music lyrics from the eras herein referenced would readily bear this thesis out). This, too, is testimony to the power of the musical medium, and it creates the inroad that the enemy needs to infect the next generation with his corruption.

This principle was poignantly demonstrated at last years Grammy awards. The president of the Academy for Recording Arts and Sciences, Michael Greene, made a speech defending the decision to include a performance by controversial Rap star, Eminem, whose expressions include murderous lyrics and other blatant profanities. The reasoning of the most powerful entertainment society in the world was that, since our generation's parents didn't like the Beatles (our musical vice), we could not judge an act such as Eminem (the current musical vice). The logic of this argument is actually air tight, albeit by now grossly cliched. Once you've started down the road to compromise, you can't complain about where it may lead. When it is evident that we have not truly repented of our own depravities, the following generation gets the go-ahead to 'out-do' us with theirs.

True repentance would therefore include a thorough housecleaning aimed at eliminating the remnants of moral corruption, destroying—not recycling—the offending items. God commands us to "take away the accursed thing from among you" (Josh. 7:13). Then and only then will we see more clearly to "remove the beam" from the eyes of others.

-The righteous audience bears guilt for a failure of vigilance in maintaining a righteous standard and a corresponding lack of respect and support for the medium of music. The world promotes and rewards its artisans, as their astounding salaries testify. However, getting any compensation as a skilled player in a sacred setting is now a rare occurrence. The statement "it is the heart that counts" is often given to support the use of the mediocre, but a slap in the face feels the same, no matter the intent. The world knows this and therefore is not attracted to our expressions, more often than not. If the musical art is a legitimate profession, and it is, then its practitioners need to be treated accordingly. Christian organizations might also consider offering 'grants' for serious sacred music composition, something the world does as a matter of course, rather than merely lamenting about the sad state of the arts.

-Spiritual leaders have displayed a lack of education and appreciation of the musical art and must shoulder some responsibility. What if talents such as Mozart, Beethoven, or Elvis had not been driven from the church in order to exercise their considerable talents, but rather had been supported and encouraged to carry the biblical message? If great music adds credibility to a false message, what effect can it have on a presentation of truth?

The Bible tells us of the future of the ungodly music of our day. In describing the fall of (Mystery) Babylon the Great,[1] the prophet records, "The sound of harpists,

---

[1] Notice the similarity between Babylon and 'Avalon', a thinly veiled 'code-word' that portrays a mythical occult legend and one that some professing Christian artists, perhaps naively, associate with.

musicians, flutists, and trumpeters shall not be heard in you anymore" (Rev. 18:22). Though for His purposes, the Sovereign Lord allows rebellion to continue, and even reign for a time, that time is most definitely measured.

The 'Mark'

Now consider the well-known prophecy addressing the end-time economic system of the AntiChrist;

"And that no one may buy or sell except one who has the *mark* or the name of the beast, or the *number* of his name. Here is wisdom. Let him who has understanding calculate the number of the beast, for it is the number of a man: *His number is 666*" [Ital. added] (Rev. 13: 17-18).

As a visual reminder of the commercial sellout of our culture, we have the omnipresent bar-code, which adorns every modern-day purchase. Now a part of the cover art of the recording, it is a testimonial to the submission of the art to the materialistic forces of today's marketplace. A recording of musical art (C.D.) is now treated no differently than a box of Wheaties (or imagine a Picasso or a Rembrandt being bar-coded). Not only is this stamp an unsightly intrusion into the sacred space that should be reserved for the artist and his following, a more sinister explanation may be relevant.

Three 'control delimiters' are to be found within the coding of each of the UPC codes on products today. The numbers that accompany the other delimiters are missing from the middle and end bars. These bars, numbered according to their respective widths, represent the number six. (Compare these bars to those that sit atop a 'six' on any given product). Defenders of the bar-code system claim that the delimiters don't represent numbers, and that their similar appearance to the bar that represents a six is "coincidental." They also mock the practice of looking for the hidden 666 by showing ludicrous examples such as turning the word "giggle" upside down (a lower case 'g' can be made to look like an upside-down '6') to reveal the AntiChrist number. An interesting mockery until you observe that one does not need to associate with the word "giggle" to participate in world-wide buying and selling today.

Omitted control numbers of UPC bar-code.

The Greek word for mark is *charagma* meaning an "etching" or "stamp." Anyone attending a modern concert or club venue is familiar with the requisite *stamp on the right hand* as standard admittance procedure. The wearing of tattoos has now become a familiar symbol of the pop culture, being promoted in large part by music stars boasting them on various parts of their anatomy. What could all this be preparing us for? Now consider the following poignant illustration from a newspaper in Boulder, Colorado, the high-tech center of the West, relating to a recent story on the advancing I.D. tracking technology.

Music, Spirit, and the Keys to Prophecy

The Boulder Weekly, Sept. 2000
Newspaper cover from Boulder, Colorado,

The Russian 'Orthodox' Church recently debated for three days before declaring that the bar-code does not conceal the "number of the beast." However it was reported that the debate was of such a heated nature that at one point "schism was threatened."[1]

The godless materialists appear to be advancing their agenda in the realm of internet commerce as well. All web addresses begin with the prefix "www," an acronym for "world wide *web*" (words do mean things). The sixth letter of the Hebrew alphabet is the *vav*, the ancient Hebrew equivalent of a "w." Thus another hidden 666 is found on the modern commercial landscape, and is also associated with buying and selling, and a technology which of its own right must raise our suspicions to some extent.

In the marketplace of today it is practically impossible to 'sell' without the use of the bar-code. All that is left then

---

[1] EP News Service, *Colorado Christian Chronicle* June, 2001.

to fulfill the prophecy is to require a bar-code like tattoo or stamp (perhaps invisible ink), or subcutaneous implant on the right hand or forehead that is then connected to worship (Greek, "to bow or do reverence," perhaps before a scanner) and buying. The use of such technology would eliminate the need for carrying the various credit cards and IDs that are increasingly necessary in society today. It would on the surface appear to be a good idea. Additionally, if the current threat of chemical and biological warfare turns into a disease epidemic, as many fear, the move to a cashless society could be seen as a necessity. Our currency, when exchanged between individuals, can facilitate the spread of disease. With something like the smallpox virus on the loose, this method of currency exchange could be deadly, facilitating the move to a "cashless society." Biblically, however, such a move may also involve submission to the 'beast' and lost hope of salvation for its willing participants (Rev 14:11). This is an interesting possibility to observe and a call to artists and audience alike to pick up their prophetic mantles and begin resisting such encroachments on the sanctity of the creative, spiritual, and cultural domain as is represented in the bar-code, what it symbolizes, and conceals. The challenge echoed from New Testament times on was never more urgent:

> "The battle is between Christ and AntiChrist . . . 'Choose ye this day whom you will serve.'" [1]

---

[1] Austin, H.W. 'Bunny.' *Frank Buchman as I Knew Him*, Grosvenor Books, London, 1975.

The Performance Medium

In facing the best and worst of possibilities that we are afforded today, we must put the various elements of the musical experience into proper context to understand and to best choose from the options available: electronic music verses acoustic, live or recorded, or a combination of all the above. The music lover of today is faced with deceptive and sometimes confusing choices. Each has some benefit with an accompanying detriment. As in all matters of life, laxity in our choices will always afford us the least appealing possibility.

Acoustic vs. Electronic music

The complexity of choices available to the performer and listener in instrument selection is phenomenal in our day. Every conceivable variation is virtually at the fingertips of any modern performer due to the advanced state of modern technology. Wisdom and caution are indicated in making the best possible choices, however.

By definition, acoustic music uses the natural elements in producing musical tones. The artist interacts directly with wood, metals, animal skins (drums), the human voice, and the like to produce and amplify tones. The quality of the performance is dependent upon the condition of the artist, his instrument and the hall where the music is being produced. The sonic vibrations are the purest and most naturally conveyed to the audience, and the artist has the greatest feel and response from his instrument in this ideal. The instrument produces not only the fundamental pitch of the note being played, but also a rich combination of overtones, giving a multidimensional experience of the sound to the listener.

In electronic music the tone is either produced through synthesis, sampling (playing back a recorded sound), or acoustically with an electronic pickup placed near the tone-producing device. The means of amplification is artificial and depends on a number of technological variables including the quality of the electronics and of the abilities of those engineering the sound. Though the audio reproduction of the sound is often quite good, there is a noticeable lack of vibration from the instrument both for the artist and the audience.[1] In sampling and synthesis, the fundamental pitch that is produced may be quite accurate to the original except that the complex 'overtone series' produced by different frequencies interacting in nature is missing. A close replica is possible, but ultimately the result of synthesis is, by comparison, stale.

Most live music today is some combination of both acoustic and electronic sound with pre-recorded sounds being increasingly used in 'popular' music venues. Concerts performed on acoustic instruments today usually involve some electronic enhancement in delivery to the audience and monitoring to the artist. This allows for larger venues than otherwise possible. There are also vast potentials for abuse in the absence of skillful production, including hearing loss, and generally unpleasant seating and crowd control methods. Rarely is pure acoustic music performed today except within a classical music context.

---

[1] Modern jazz pianist Keith Jarrett, an acoustic music advocate, claims that electronic instruments are a "physical irritant." Actually with the use of recording and amplification technology, even his performances become 'electronic' to some extent.

Live vs. Recorded

To overlook the important differences between the live and the recorded music experience is like not distinguishing between a real landscape and a mere painting.

Live music is by its nature of the moment. Each performance is unique and honest, and responds to the various elements of performance. These elements primarily include the mental, physical and emotional state of the artist, and his abilities to interact with the audience, as well as his instrument, and his chosen repertoire. Successful performance is also dependent on the audience, on the sponsorship of the venue, and the venue itself. As all these elements work together to make a live show, this performance medium has the greatest potential for creating the most honest human connections.

Recorded music, by contrast, reflects on 'one moment in time' and is replayed indefinitely at the hearer's request. Once the performance is recorded and purchased, (or often times *acquired)*, it is out of the performer's hands. The quality of the recording is contingent upon the variables existing at the time of the recording plus the availability and use of production and editing technology. With the advent of recording technology the true performing *profession* in music virtually died. As technology has advanced through the years this effect has become more and more a reality.

Many of the live performance venues now use some level of recorded tracks to enhance their performances without the added expense and trouble of live players. Recorded music also typically involves a considerable amount of signal processing such as compression, limiting, and electronic reverberation. The direct interaction between artist and audience is non-existent and the potential for unhealthy uses and abuses are thereby greatly increased. It should be understood that a recorded performance is not music in the truest sense, but only a sonic *photograph*.

With regard to artist compensation, we cannot here adequately discuss all the complexities of creative rights issues. Suffice it to say that internet technology may ultimately deal the final fatal blow for the performing artist. Without the backing of major concert promoters and with the increasingly free access to pirated recordings via the internet, the artist is now literally the *slave* to his audience. Acting as a true Judas Iscariot, recording technology, which first served to *deify* the artist, now stands ready to *crucify* him.

Those concerned parties who are involved in the various aspects of the art—from artist to producer to listener—should carefully consider their uses of the available possibilities of today. Great benefits may be enjoyed but one should respect the needs of all involved in the process. Technology, here as elsewhere, is beneficial only when utilized and controlled by a knowledgeable and moral people. As stated in the introductory section, music is primarily about intimacy and, as with sexual relations, *intimacy without commitment is fraud*.

Conclusion

If you have read this far, you have come to know of things that have escaped studied people throughout history. You have apprehended some of the truths of the ancient outlook that saw the various disciplines of life as connecting to each other and, most importantly, to God. You have also seen significant new proof that the musical art is intimately connected to the Almighty in ways not previously understood, and that music in its purest sense, is an expression of praise and glory unto the LORD.

Also, in studying the events and meaning of the Apocalypse, we find our return to the ancient path with the Second Coming of Christ and the setting up of His government on the earth. Once again men will comprehend that all things are connected to each other and most importantly to God. Knowledge of His sovereignty over the earth and of His judgments will once again permeate every culture and men will retain these understandings from generation to generation. The deceivers who would obscure such knowledge will be subjugated under foot, re-emerging only one last time at the end of the Millennial Reign, and then forever banished from God's presence.

In the light of such understanding, I would encourage each to consider the personal acceptance of His provision—completed in the person and sacrifice of *Yeshua HaMeshiach* (Jesus, the Christ), who is the only door to the Almighty. That you will then continue with a deepening surrender to His will, by reflection on personal sin, contemplation of His revealed truth, and all such means of disciplined worship. I also pray that you will find a fellowship of spiritual and committed people with whom to grow, and that you continue to discern the times leading up to the Lord's soon return.

"I am the door. If anyone enters by Me, he will be saved, and will go in and out and find pasture. "The thief does not come except to steal, and to kill, and to destroy. I have come that they may have life, and that they may have it more abundantly." John 10:9-10

Appendix I

The *Music of Creation*: Apologetic and Analysis
By R.S. James

*Note: It has been historically accepted in both Christian and Jewish traditions that there exist differing levels of scriptural interpretation. This article represents a previously unknown area as well as an historical *first*. In the future, I believe we will come to commonly accept and appreciate studies that are dedicated to gaining a more complete understanding of the scriptures through *the performance and analysis of its music.*

Apologetic:

The idea that the Hebrew Bible came to us with music is news to most people today. Partly responsible is the fact that, despite the many evidences and proofs supporting the claim, most scholars are reluctant even to address the issue. However, if one takes time to sufficiently explore this music itself, they will find here perhaps the most compelling evidence.

The melodic rendering for the composition, "Chant: The Creation," is according to the only musical and self-consistent approach to the cantorial markings (*te`amim*) in existence. A difficult study, to be sure, even for those with the necessary musical and linguistic skills to master the notation, this system has remained relatively unknown since its development by French musicologist Suzanne Haik-Vantoura some twenty-five years ago.

In attempting to work with this music, one encounters several other formidable roadblocks. Superstitious beliefs capture those who would maintain that anything but absolute *purity* in the ancient expressions is out of the question, no matter how inaccessible that may be to the vast majority of listeners. It has been well observed that the biblical verbal syntax itself developed and was modernized as it went through the succeeding generations of ancient Israel. This is a principle that must also apply to the music.

Those calling for such purity in these expressions (ancient style, Hebrew only) must also consider the need to evangelize the modern listener.

Traditions, even non-biblical ones, die slowly as the idea of adding any accompaniment to a rendering of the Hebrew notation is considered to be 'anathema.' Here I would point to the Psalmist who, in his statement "Thy statutes have been my *songs*" (Ps. 119:54), used the Hebrew word *zimerot* (Strong's # 2158), meaning *accompanied* melodies.

Here, then, is an unabashed rebel, yet not one without impressive results. The piano is used, a modern extension of the harp, to carry the musical improvisation of Genesis 1—not unlike great jazz—to the modern ear. The English narration is added on the principle that the audience should hear for themselves the stunning melody-to-prose relationship that exists, not just be told of it by 'experts' (of which there are few). The integrity of acoustic performance is maintained, and the notation and text are faithfully rendered. With these advances the piece is on sound footing with the authors being interpreted and with the modern audience. The ethic is thus upheld, that there is not "old or new" music, but there is only, as the great jazz composer Duke Ellington stated, "good or bad music."

Having established a case for the legitimacy of the arrangement in question, what follows are some observations on the biblical melody and narrative themselves.

A Musical 'Midrash'

To take a closer look at the way the melodies of scripture lend to and establish the meaning of the sacred text, we shall use a prime example, the Creation account from Genesis 1.

Stylistically, this melody reflects what is commonly seen throughout the Mosaic revelation. It is a bold and confident melodic style that gets 'right to the point' and carries the no-nonsense spirit of these great doctrines. The opening phrase of this epic narrative, "In the beginning created God (*Elohim*)," is stated with a most appropriate major tonic triad, conveying the grandeur of the statement. The musical phrase then comes to a point of rest on the modal subdominant (the fourth) coinciding with the word *Elohim*, i.e., a resting on the plurality of the Godhead! The matching of melodic and verbal phrases continues as such throughout the narration, with the music always resting appropriate to the verbal thought. This demonstrates also how the musical notation functions as punctuation within the Hebrew text.

A decisive proof of the system is found in the recurrent phrase *va yomer Elohim,* "and God said . . ." The *trumpet call*, or rising-fifth interval, is known throughout scripture and history as that which is used to awaken our attention to important ideas and events. Here we find this interval employed to announce the Word of the Lord, preceding all but one of the ten declarations of the Almighty during the Creation week. This demonstrates a consistency of theology within the music itself. (As you listen your ear will clearly identify this devise.)

The next point of interest comes with the enumeration of the days of the week. A well-known verbal 'hook' is used for all six days of creation, "and the evening and the morning were the (1st-6th) day." With each repetition, an identical melodic motif is employed, creating a sonic unifying factor throughout the narrative. Within this phrase another effective devise is also employed. The dark-sounding interval of the minor 2nd leads to the word *erev* (evening), and expands to a 'bright' major third interval for the word *voker* (day), displaying amazingly detailed usage of this altered scale and musical imagery. Similarly, motivic cadences are repeated for the recurrent phrases "and it was so," and "and God saw that it was good." Such would be considered great song-writing, in any era.

Another compositional device that is used to great effect is that of the 'melodic ornament.' Here the fundamental pitch used for selected words is embellished in order to create emphasis and/or a tonal picture of the action being stated. This occurs variously with such important verbal concepts as the earth bringing forth *grass* and *fruit trees* (v. 11), man being given *dominion* on the earth (v. 26), and God saying to *behold* His gifts (v.29).

By now we have the sense that this is far more than just a 'formula' chant used to put some tonal inflection into the readings of scripture as in the traditional systems of interpretation. Rather, this is a true work of art, creating a new *dimension* to the scriptures altogether, all the while respecting and enhancing the poetry of the sacred text.

For a final punctuation of this effect, we come to the seventh day and God's rest from His Creative works. Here we find a broadening and slowing of the fast-paced musical ideas that accompanied the other six days. Ultimately we come to rest with God "from all His work" (Gen. 2:3) on the modal tonic itself, a true spiritual and musical Sabbath.

Glossary of Terms

Midrash- "a drawing out" of a hidden or not readily apparent meaning from a passage of scripture.

Musical Terms

Tonic triad- A chord built on the final resting pitch of a scale.

Subdominant- Fourth degree of the scale, a place of temporary rest.

Motif- A short melodic idea.

Interval- The distance between tones of the scale.

Modal- The particular scale type used in a given composition.

Melodic Ornament- An embellishment to a fundamental pitch within the melodic line.

5 Biblical Weeks
The "Fugue" of God

The 'fugue' is the most intricately woven and precisely crafted of musical compositions. It is form of imitative counterpoint wherein a particular *theme* is played in different voices that variously overlap, and that play in different registers and rhythmic lengths, and so on. A canon such as "row, row, row, your boat" demonstrates the simplest of these techniques. Fugues typically vary from three, four, and five "voices," as is gloriously demonstrated in Bach's "Well-Tempered Clavier." The fugue is also known to separate "the men from the boys" as composers. Among the masters of this art are Bach, Mozart, and Beethoven.

In view of the following summary chart, the fugue is also perhaps the best analogy in all of artistic endeavor to portray the reality of the biblical drama as it plays itself out through the course of history. By 'playing' the *themes* of the biblical week in stages, at different and overlapping times, with the weeks being different in their lengths, and through various peoples, God ensures that His will is being played out upon the earth. Most accurately, the biblical drama is a five-voice fugue, its principle dramatic theme utilizing the seven-day 'week.' Two 'types' reflect the governing principles of the drama and they are: the yearly feast cycle, and the seven-fold Spirit. The seven divine covenants (see footnote, pg. 27) also parallel the feast cycle and the seven-fold spirit.

Thus, quite literally, the biblical drama is the "fugue of God."

Music, Spirit, and the Keys to Prophecy

Right to left = Parallels within the biblical dramas. Look for key words and similarities in dramatic imagery.
Verticle = progression of the days through the dramatic tonal and spiritual sequence (see the scale type, chap.4, 9 for scripture references; also see the 7-fold Spirit, and the Week of Biblical Feasts.)

Day	Creation Week	Human History 1 day=1k yr	Crucifixion Week
1	Heaven & Earth, light & dark created. Center of story is defined.	Life of Adam. People heavenly or earthly (light or dark).	Christ enters Jerusalem, "peace in Heaven," palm branches.
2	*Waters* separated	World-wide *flood* separates (judges) peoples.	Christ teaches faith can cast mtn. into *sea*
3	Waters gathered into "one place" Vegetation created.	Moses and law People gathered to Sinai, promised land (one place)	People gather into Temple (one place) to hear Christ teach.
4	Lights in the heavens for signs, seasons, and years.	Babylonian captivity for Israel, trials.	Son of God is tried, struck.
5	Living creatures created and blessed.	*Life* giving atonement of the cross. Purity	Christ put into earth, given keys to hell. *Life* through the cross.
6	Man and beast made and blessed	Man populates and *dominates* the earth. "Beast" empires arise. Sabbath prep. through Tribulation.	Christ descends, *dominates* hell & death. Apostles prepare for Sabbath.
7	God rests from Creation. *Storms* of human history on earth.	Millenial Reign of Christ, earth rests. Last Satan-led rebellion (*storm*).	Apostles rest. Christ resurrected. earthquake.
8 Resolutions	Eternal State: New Heavens and New Earth		First-fruits, Resurrection revealed.

Appendix II: The Biblical "Fugue"

Tribulation Seals (Years)	Trumpet Judg.
Peace treaty "olive branch" w/ Israel & AntiChrist.	Trees and grass (earth 'gods') are burned.
Peace taken, people kill each other (separation)	Burning mtn. (Torah) cast into *sea* (people)
Scales (law of Anti Christ) Believers (oil and wine, liquid) protected.	Star falls makes waters bitter (one third.
Moon (believers) stars (Israel) struck.	Sun, moon, stars struck.
Martyrs purified, receive eternal life.	Star falls, keys to hell given. Ungodly harmed.
Dominion of earth changing, fire, smoke. 144k 'prepared'	Fire, smoke, brim. 1/3 *man*kind killed. Final prep. For Sabbath Mill.
Censer thrown, storms. Trumpets sound prepare earth for Mill.	Begins the Sabbath Mill. Thunder, lightning. Armaggedon.
Millennial Kingdom	Second Advent

Two more biblical 'weeks' are consistent with the dramatic principles of the musical scale. These are the week of the biblical feasts, and the Menorah representing the seven-fold Spirit of God. These, however, do not 'resolve' as do the previous weeks because they are eternal ordinances and principles, not specific dramas in themselves.

	Biblical Feasts	7-Fold Spirit
1	*Rosh HaShana*, Trumpets Head of the year, birthdate of Adam, Christ.	*Spirit of the Lord*, Creator of all things. Central focus of all creation.
2	*Yom Kippur* "Day of Atonement" (Waters divided, flood, etc.)	*Wisdom*, separation of good from evil.
3	Tabernacles (Waters gathered, giving of the Torah)	*Understanding*, People gathered and instructed.
4	*Passover (Disciples scattered, Crucifixion)	*Counsel*, lights created for signs, seasons, also trials.
5	First Fruits (Resurrection revealed)	*Might*, Comes from purity, atonement.
6	Pentecost, *Shavuot* (Spirit poured into man)	*Knowledge*, Man (6) develops and increases in knowledge in 6th millennium.
7	Sabbath (Rest) (Also storms as subplot until Eternal State)	*Fear of the Lord*, Fear of Lord is theme of each Sabbath and result of each weeks events.

Appendix II: The Biblical "Fugue"

Feasts of the LORD Trumpets, Day of Atonement, Tabernacles, Passover,* First Fruits, Pentecost, and the Sabbath. (Leviticus 23)

The feasts may also be reckoned beginning at Passover and continuing to Shavuot and the Sabbath. The principles in this case would still be parallel. The feasts are likewise reckoned one of these two ways depending upon whether one is starting the Jewish "Civil" or the "Religious" calendar.

*The Passover feast is an eight-day week, including the seven days of unleavened bread. This emphasizes the Crucifixion week of Christ, which culminated on the eighth day and fulfilled not only the theme of the Passover, but also addressed the respective themes of the days of the Creation week (a correction to the Fall).

In an exact parallel, the seven-note scale has seven primary modes, (7x7) which, as this book has demonstrated, also parallel thematically the biblical weeks (7x7). Hebrew grammar also has 7 known verb 'moods' (called *binyanim*).

In observing the biblical symbolism, God seeing people as water is quite accurate. The human body is made up of approximately 70% water weight, the rest 'clay.' This is also the same proportion of water to land on the earth.

Believers in God are metaphorically referred to in scripture as oil. Oil is produced when organic matter (the other 30% of the body) is placed under *intense pressure and heat* (tribulation).

Oil, when mixed with water, *separates and rises to the top,* the same results that one expects as God's people interact with society.

7-fold Spirit of God "The Spirit of the LORD shall rest upon Him, The Spirit of wisdom and understanding, The Spirit of counsel and might, The Spirit of knowledge and of the fear of the LORD." (Isa. 11:2)

The seven-fold spirit is the dramatic 'template' and therefore the progressive process of maturity by which the weeks of scripture, the musical scale, and even personal spiritual growth function.

All dramas begin with the *Spirit of the LORD* as their central focus, or beginning (tonic) note. It is here that the spiritual walk begins and that the main theme of the drama is established. Next comes *wisdom*, which always challenges the status quo and creates a separation from the things of the world. Through wisdom we learn to discern between good and evil, and between the things of our former life and the new spiritual direction.

From wisdom we come to a place of *understanding*. By being gathered for instruction in the ways of God, and studying His word, we begin to undertake the spiritual learning process. In music, it is the third scale degree that helps us to understand the modality of the piece. The fourth is *counsel* wherein we are variously tried and exposed to the light to reveal what imperfections may still exist. The discordant blue-note is an altered sound that mirrors the trials of God's people during this stage of growth, both personally and throughout history.

By enduring the purification of trials during the stage of counsel, we develop *might*. The number five is that of purity and grace, and musically it is intermediate rest as well as a strong and pure interval. *Knowledge* is the result of adding experience with instruction. It is the action of utilizing the strength received through our trials, and putting spiritual instruction into practice. Earthly dominion and the sixth manifestation of the Spirit, or the super-dominant, come only after heavenly dominion has been accomplished at the fifth stage. It is only by exposure to the preceding workings of the Spirit that one is allowed to participate at this level. The dominion of the earth, through knowledge was the theme of the sixth day of the Creation week and of all successive weeks.

Appendix II: The Biblical "Fugue"

The seventh manifestation of the Spirit is *the fear of the LORD*, the Sabbath that we come to after the events of the preceding week. The beginning theme of the week is restated, yet with a maturity that results from the experience of the week's events. In the biblical weeks there is also the sub-plot of storms at the end of each Sabbath, propelling us into the drama of a new week's events. As in the musical scale we resolve to the octave, or the beginning of a new drama, replaying the principles of the seven-fold Spirit at a higher level, except in the Eternal State, when we reach the final ascension of all time.

7 Divine Covenants of the Bible: 1) Edenic-The Garden before the fall, sets the tone-fear of the Lord. **2) Abrahamic**-Crossing from polytheism. Challenges the status quo, wisdom/separation. **3) Mosaic**-Establishes mood, people gathered for instruction. **4) Jehoichinic**-The Babylonian captivity, discord/trials/counsel. **5) Messianic**-Crucifixion of Christ. Purity/intermediate rest. **6) Millenial Kingdom**-Christ's reign on earth. Earthly dominion. **7) Eternal State**-New Heavens and New Earth. Fear of the Lord/True Sabbath rest.

An Eternal Ethic

We thus may add to, and further clarify the answer to the age-old question of what the purpose of music ought to be. Aristotle taught that "art imitates nature." Yet for Bach, art "lay between the reality of the world—nature—and God, who ordered this reality . . . Music is a mixed mathematical science that concerns the origins, attributes, and distinctions of sound, out of which a cultivated and lovely melody and harmony are made, so that God is honored and praised but mankind is moved to devotion, virtue, joy, and sorrow." [1]

---

[1] Wolff, Christoff. *Johann Sebastian Bach: The Learned Musician.* New York W.W Norton and Co. p.5.

In truth, music serves an even deeper and more literal truth than even Bach understood. As this book has shown, music symbolically plays the major themes of the biblical drama, and audibly represents Christ Himself. It is then the skillful working out of this symbolism through the tonal drama for the purpose of magnifying and glorifying the Creator that is the ethic toward which all music must be aimed. This is a literal truth beyond what the most studied musicians of the past were able to comprehend.

Music, as the scriptures command, and as history bears witness, is also to be carried out by *skilled and holy artisans*. The musician is ultimately handling, in the physics of musical tonality, the symbolic representation of Christ and the Bible, and must perform their work in accordance with such a calling. These artisans, in turn, need to be supported by their respective communities. The careless and common expressions that are so prevalent today, should not be promoted under the auspices of following popular trends, or for the sake of mere convenience. God truly deserves our best in this area.

Conversely, the misdirected efforts of the many talented people throughout history who, lacking discernment, corrupted music's sacred purpose, as well as those forces that taint this purpose with materialistic, impure, and Godless messages, must likewise be supplanted. In this way, music will be restored to its highest God-intended purpose.

The musical art may then gloriously serve the wide range of uses that are reflected in the scriptures, both edifying man and glorifying God. May this study be a step towards that goal, for His glory, and in His power.

Praise be to the LORD for all of His wondrous works,
forever. Amen

Glossary of Musical Terms

Accidentals- Alterations to a given pitch by a half-step using flats, sharps, and naturals not contained in the key signature.

Atonal- Lit., "absence of tonality." Music from the 20th century typified by lack of a key center.

Counterpoint- The art of adding one or more parts to a given part—the combination into a single musical fabric of lines or parts which have distinctive melodic significance.*

Chromatic- The use of tones extraneous to the diatonic scale.* The scale made up of all twelve notes within the octave.

Diatonic- The natural scale consisting of five whole tones and two semitones, as is produced by the white keys of the keyboard.*

Fugue- The latest and most mature form of imitative counterpoint, developed during the 17th century and brought to its highest perfection by J.S. Bach.*

Half step- The small distance between two conjoint scale degrees.

Harmony- When two or more voices sound at different, yet complementary pitches. A chord.

Interval- The difference in pitch between two tones. Indicated by the number of the tones of the diatonic scale included therein.

Liturgy- Officially authorized service of sacred music.

Micro-tonal- Any interval smaller than a semitone, or half-step.

Mode- The selection of tones, arranged in a scale, which form the basic tonal substance of a composition. Determine the mood of piece, whether major, minor, or altered scales.*

Motif- The briefest intelligible and self-contained fragment of a musical theme or subject.* A musical thought or idea.

Ornament- An alteration to a given pitch. The spontaneous act in performing a written or traditional melody, to enliven, expand, or vary through improvisation.
Tonic- The principle note of a key or mode, the center point of attraction of a melody or piece.
Twelve-tone music- A system of composition, devised mainly by Arnold Schonberg as an attempt to take the place of traditional principles of tonality.* The 12 chromatic tones are treated as of equal importance.
Unison- Two or more voices or instruments sounding at the same pitch or in a different octave.

* *Harvard Dictionary of Music*. By Willi Apel. Harvard University Press. Cambridge, Massachusetts. 1960.

Order Form

Books

☐ *Music, Spirit, and the Keys to Prophecy* $19.95
    by R.S. James

☐ Book and tape special $24.95

Recordings

☐ The Music of the Prophets   C.D. $14.95
    by Roger James

☐ *Chant: The Creation* from Genesis 1
original music of the Creation
w/ narration and overview   Cassette $7.95

Add $4.25 S&H. + $1.00 ea additional copy. Out of U.S. $5.00/ $3.00 (addl. copies). In Colorado add 3.8% tax. Check or money order, payable to the Twiggs Company. Please allow three to six weeks delivery. Thank you for your order. Call (720) 275-7647 for volume discount schedule or information.

Total Order $_____	Name _____
Shipping $_____	Address _____
$_____	_____
	Phone#_____
Total $_____	e-mail_____

Send To:
   Sacred Scales
   1135A Big Thompson Canyon
   Loveland, Colorado 80538

ide U.S. & Canada)

..... ooo-o41-0020
www.sacredscales.com